CANNIBAL TROUT

TYING & FISHING FLESH, FRY AND EGG FLIES

Andrew Williams

The Lakelse is a wonderful place to meet new friends. Andrew.

CANNIBAL TROUT

TYING & FISHING FLESH, FRY AND EGG FLIES

Andrew Williams

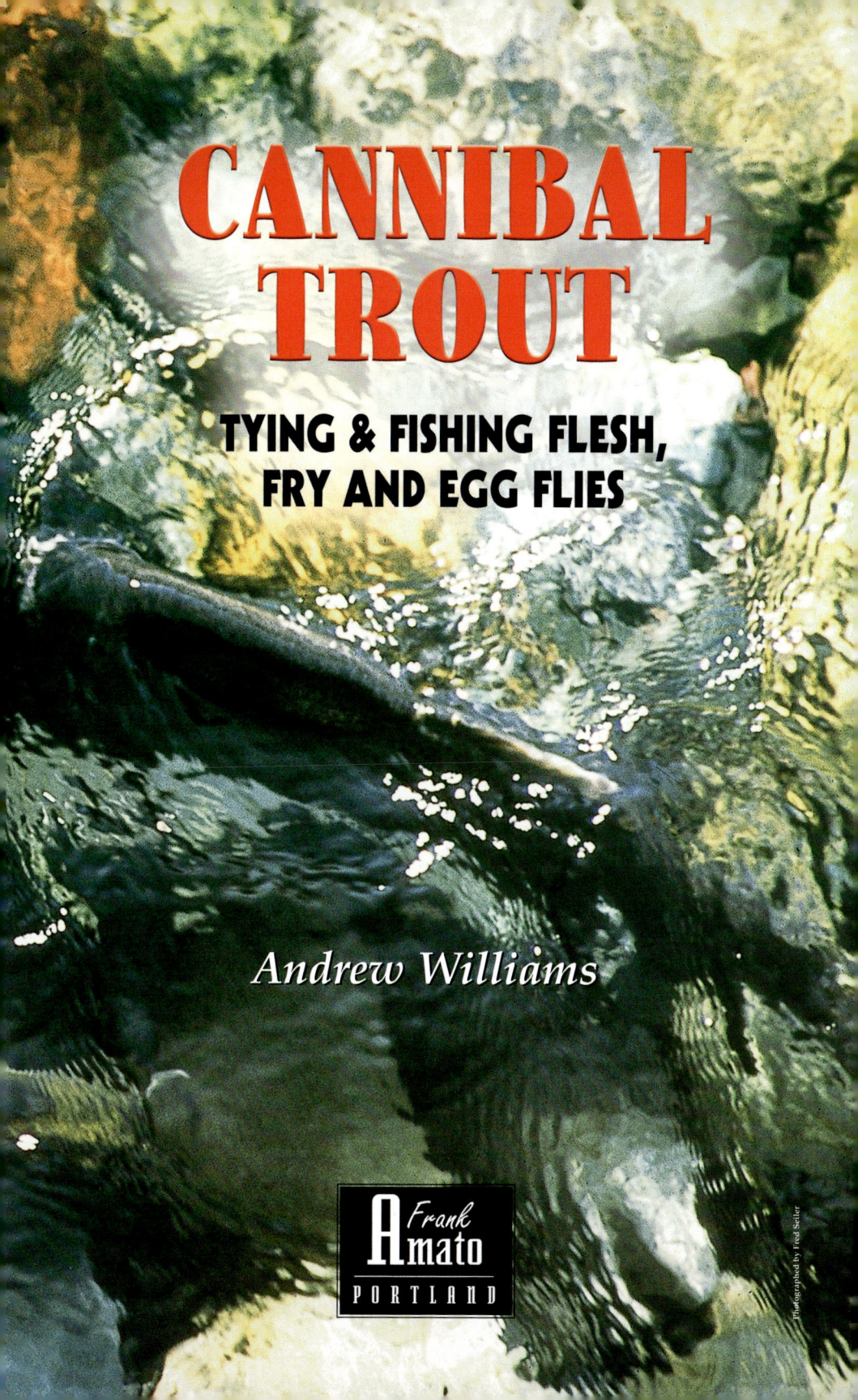

Frank Amato
PORTLAND

DEDICATION

*"For Rhian and Janine:
thanks for all your patience while dad fished."*

ANDREW WILLIAMS

Although he was born in England near the famous Itchen and Test rivers, Andrew Williams didn't take up fly-fishing until the day he pulled a fly rod and reel out of the Ausable River in upper New York State. The passion that was born that day led him to being the founding president of the Ottawa Fly Fishers in Ontario, and to fly-fish in the United Kingdom, eastern Canada and New England.

In 1989, he moved to the banks of the Kispiox River in northern British Columbia and found a new addiction—steelhead. He worked with the Steelhead Society of BC on the Wild Steelhead Campaign to reduce the impact of commercial salmon fishing on the Skeena River's precious steelhead. Since then, he has lived in the north, fishing, teaching and writing for various American and Canadian fly-fishing magazines. He is chairman of Friends of Wild Salmon, a group dedicated to protecting the wild salmon and steelhead of the Pacific Northwest.

© 2005 Andrew Williams
All rights reserved. No part of this book may be
reproduced in any means without the written consent of the publisher,
except in the case of brief excerpts in critical reviews and articles.

Published in 2005 by
Frank Amato Publications, Inc.
PO Box 82112 • Portland, Oregon 97282 • (503) 653-8108
Softbound ISBN: 1-57188-380-0 • Softbound UPC: 0-81127-00214-6

All photographs taken by author, unless otherwise noted
Illustrations by Andrew Williams
Book Design: Leslie Brannan
Printed in Hong Kong

1 3 5 7 10 9 8 6 4 2

CONTENTS

Introduction: Page 6
Born to Spawn
The Important Role of the Pacific Salmon
in the Rivers and Forests of the Northwest

Chapter One: Page 11
The Life Cycles
of the Pacific Salmon

Chapter Two: Page 16
Spring Time
The Features of the Salmon Alevin, Fry and Smolts,
and Tying Flies to Imitate Them

Chapter Three: Page 41
Fishing Salmon Alevin
Fry and Smolt "Hatches"

Chapter Four: Page 62
Salmon Caviar
The Moveable Feast

Chapter Five: Page 68
Fishing Egg Patterns

Chapter Six: Page 70
Salmon Flesh
Tying and Fishing its Imitation

Additional Flies: Page 78
Match the Salmon Hatches

INTRODUCTION

Born to Spawn

Every year, adult pink, sockeye, chum, coho, and chinook salmon battle upstream in coastal rivers from California to Alaska, often travelling hundreds of miles to complete their mating rituals on the gravel beds where they were born. Unlike their Atlantic cousins, not one of the millions of Pacific salmon that spawn in these rivers will survive to return to the ocean. Even before they have dug their redds and laid their eggs, their bodies are disfigured by the marks of death: ragged fins and patches of white bacteria. Soon, they will weaken and, unable to fight the currents any longer, begin to drift weakly downstream to die. Finally, their pale, rotting carcases will carpet the river bottoms and wave like pennants from the sunken branches that have snagged them.

Spawning chum salmon.

Photographed by Fred Seiler

When I first moved west to live on the Kispiox River, I marvelled at the bounty of nature as a seemingly endless stream of salmon, especially pinks, flowed past in late summer. Nowhere back East had I ever seen so many large fish in a river. It was easy to appreciate how the rich culture of the aboriginal peoples of the Northwest had been made possible by this abundant and reliable source of food which swam up to their villages every year. Later, however, as I witnessed the slow deterioration and final death of these hordes, the life cycle of the Pacific salmons seemed to me to be brutally ephemeral and even wasteful. Finally, the marvel of abundance was forgotten in the fall as I prayed for the rains to come and wash away the tens of thousands of carcasses that filled the air with the smell of decay.

But appearances are deceiving, and later I came to realize that what had seemed at first to be a tragic waste is in fact a noble sacrifice. The return of the salmon to their home rivers to spawn and die has been for thousands of years the foundation of the health of the entire Pacific Northwest ecosystem. By tracking the concentrations of marine-derived isotopes, nitrogen-15 and carbon-13, in plants and animals in the river valleys, fisheries biologists have found that the nutrients from salmon carcasses enrich what would otherwise be a mineral-poor, unproductive environment. In the rivers and lakes where salmon transport these nutrients, the growth and abundance of everything from algae and aquatic insects to juvenile salmon is enhanced. From the valley bottoms to the mountain tops, the great rainforests of the Northwest

Grizzly bear eating salmon.

and the creatures that live there depend on the return of the salmon.

For example, researchers Charlie Robbins and Grant Hildebrand studied museum specimens of grizzly bears from the Columbia River area, a population that has been extinct since 1931, and discovered that up to 90 per cent of the carbon and nitrogen in the bones and hair of these long-dead bears had come from salmon. They concluded that every Columbia River grizzly they had tested had fed on salmon, including bears that had lived 700-800 miles inland. Other researchers have found the same pattern of isotopes existing in human bones in the Interior of British Columbia, indicating that native peoples far from the ocean also relied on the bounty of the salmon runs, which in many cases are now a trickle of their former size.

Skunk cabbage in the spring.

Studies reveal that the bears themselves are a major agent in transporting the salmon nutrients from the river waters to the forests. Their feces and the decomposing fish carcasses that they and other predators drag up to 150 metres (492 feet) into the woods provide nitrogen, carbon and phosphorus to the birds, insects, animals and plant life of the rainforest. This nutrient pump provides up to 40% of the annual fertilization of some riverine ecosystems. University of Victoria biologists found that the amount of salmon left on the forest floor was equal to 4,000 kg./ha (3,500 pounds per acre) of commercial fertilizer, accounting for the massive size of streamside trees.

The authors of a recent article in Fisheries (Vol. 25, No. 1, January 2000) estimate the historic biomass of salmon returning to west coast streams was from 160 to 226 million kg. (176,370 to 286,600 tons). Sadly, overfishing by commercial fleets, damming, urbanization, and deforestation have severely reduced the number of adult salmon making it to the spawning beds to contribute their marine-derived nutrients to the freshwater ecosystems. The reduction now to 11.8 to 13.7 million kg. (13,228 to 15,432 tons) or 6-7 percent of the historic nutrient input, has contributed to the downward spiral of salmonid abundance and diversity, and added to the difficulties of rebuilding salmon and steelhead populations to self-sustaining levels. The ironic result is that salmon fry populations in these waters and the predators that feed on them have declined because there are not enough adults to make the noble sacrifice for their offspring.

The authors say, "Fisheries management has historically ignored such ecological implications of salmon spawning escapements. Harvests were regulated to provide the minimum number of spawners needed to seed the habitat. The contribution of 'surplus' salmon carcasses to the growth and survival of juvenile salmon was not considered when harvest and escapement targets were set."

A sad example of the problems this has caused is the catastrophic decline in steelhead populations in Vancouver Island rivers. The eastern shore of the island in particular has suffered from habitat destruction from urbanization and logging, and the problems this causes have been exacerbated by poor ocean survival in recent years. Because steelhead usually live in fresh water for two years, they are particularly affected by the reduction in nutrients that has resulted from the declining salmon runs. Attempts have been made elsewhere to fertilize some lakes and streams with artificial sources of phosphorus and nitrogen, and in places such as Washington State with spawned-out hatchery salmon. Similar plans are being discussed for 15 Vancouver Island rivers. Ultimately, the only viable method of rebuilding depleted salmon and steelhead stocks is to let more adult salmon return, to recycle their minerals and protein, thus supporting their own offspring.

We are slow to appreciate that nature knows best. In British Columbia, commercial fishermen and fisheries biologists talk about the ESSR fishery—the excess to salmon spawning requirements fishery. They refer to the "minimum spawning requirements" of salmon runs, as though every salmon in excess of these requirements that is not caught in the nets is a wasted salmon, or even worse, as though these salmon are "over spawning" and destroying the redds of others. This is like a logger or forester talking about "decadent old-growth forests," and saying that a tree has no value until it is cut down. These statements reflect the narrow view of nature as being valuable only if it contributes to human economic activity. They ignore the contribution that the nutrients of the salmon carcases make to the fertility of river bottom life and that even a fallen tree makes to the ecosystem by rotting and making soil, amongst other things. Both attitudes reveal our ignorance of the complexity of nature's inter-connected cycles. Slowly, however, we are coming to understand that salmon are truly forest creatures and that the forests themselves are the products of the salmon runs.

Sport fishermen, on the other hand, have long known that freshwater fish, such as cutthroat and rainbow trout, Dolly Varden, bull trout, and whitefish, rely on all stages of the salmon's life cycle for a major part of their diet. In the summer and fall, they stack up behind spawning salmon and gorge on the eggs. After the adults have died, trout will feed on the rotting flesh, sometimes tearing at a carcass like a pack of wolves. In the spring, as the newly hatched alevin emerge and turn into fry, trout and other fish go on a feeding frenzy until their bellies are so distended with the baby salmon an angler might wonder why they are even remotely interested in his fly. Even the smolts descending the rivers on their way to the sea must run a gauntlet of hungry trout.

Whereas the East coast angler has to imitate the various insect hatches in his home waters, to be successful, the trout fly-fisher of the Pacific Northwest must also learn the timings of each stage of the salmon hatches on the rivers he fishes and know how to match the eggs, fry, and flesh of the salmon that are present. Not only effective imitations of these food sources are the keys to success, but so too are a range of strategies and fishing techniques to present them where, when and how the trout expect to see them.

Fly-fishing in the coastal streams of the West is a relatively new phenomenon, perhaps a hundred years old at best. But even during its early stages, trout fishermen were realizing the importance of salmon as a source of food for their quarry. Shiny, silver streamers were fished in the spring as simple imitations of salmon fry and red chenille-bodied wet flies in the fall to represent eggs. White-winged streamers in the fall took hungry trout feeding on salmon flesh. Many of those simple flies from yesteryear will still catch fish, but anglers have developed more and more realistic patterns for all stages of the salmon hatch. Just as flies have advanced, so have equipment and fishing techniques. A successful angler knows that trying new patterns will increase his success, and that while the traditional wet-fly swing still has its place, varying the way he presents his fly to the trout will make it more likely he will find the combination that works. I hope this book will encourage you to experiment with new patterns and techniques when you try to match the salmon.

CHAPTER ONE

The Life Cycles
of the Pacific Salmon

Illustration by Andrew Williams

The Pacific salmon are members of the family of salmonids which probably traces its ancestry to the era of the dinosaurs, 150 million years ago. The earliest know fossil salmonid, Esalmodriftwoodensis, which was 55 million years old and was in all likelihood the progenitor of modern trout and salmon, was found in Eocene lake sediments just north of the Bulkley River in northern British Columbia. Today the trout, steelhead and Pacific salmon which are its modern ancestors swim in nearby rivers and lakes.

By the end of the Miocene era (24-5 million years ago) all the major branches of the subfamily Salmonidae were established, including the

Cutthroat trout with fry pattern.

grayling *Thymallus*; the char *Salvelinus*; brown trout and Atlantic salmon *Salmo*; and the Pacific trout, steelhead and salmon *Oncorhynchus*.

Cutthroat trout *O. clarki* and steelhead *O. mykiss* are considered by some fisheries biologists to be the most primitive of the Pacific salmon family because they both have forms which live their entire lives in fresh water, have limited migration patterns and may live to spawn more than once. The sea-run cutthroat trout tend to stay close to estuaries and coastlines and will enter fresh water to feed several times in the year. In spring, they feed on the emerging salmon fry and in the fall they often follow the adult salmon upriver to feed on their eggs. The timing of the different runs of steelhead varies tremendously, with some entering the rivers in the summer and fall and staying over the winter in the rivers, and others entering in spring for a few weeks only. Steelhead feed very little in fresh water. Steelhead lead extremely variable life cycles: staying in fresh water for up to three years before going to sea and returning from one to four years later. In short, coastal rivers, steelhead will return to fresh water in the spring, spawn and leave after a few weeks. In larger, inland rivers they will return in the summer and fall, over winter in fresh water, and spawn in the spring before migrating back to salt water. Some rivers even have populations that show both patterns of behaviour. The river-resident form of the steelhead is the rainbow trout which is taxonomically identical. Like their cousins the brown trout, cutthroat and rainbow trout, and steelhead are spring spawners. The record cutthroat is 40 pounds, but anything over 10 pounds today is pretty special. Steelhead over 40 pounds have been caught in commercial nets, although the average size is probably more like 13 pounds.

Coho or silvers *O. kisutch* and chinook or kings *O. tshawytscha* are considered the next most advanced after the Asian amago and cherry *O. masu* salmon because they have a long freshwater residency as smolts—one to two years. There are a few coho populations, such as those in Cultus Lake in southern B.C., that do not migrate to the ocean at all, reach sizes of only two feet or less. Some chinook do not wander far from their home rivers and return as small, immature "jacks," predominantly precocious males. Coho will spend from six months to two years in the ocean, average ten pounds at maturity, and spawn from September to December. Chinook spend up to seven years in salt water which accounts for their larger size—up to 100 pounds. They enter rivers from April to August and spawn in the late summer and early fall. Some biologists consider the most developed species of the Pacific salmon to be the chum *O. keta*, sockeye *O. nerka* and pinks *O. gorbuscha*. They have the simplest and most specialized lifestyles, rely the least on fresh water and are the most numerous of the salmon. While chum and pink fry migrate to salt water almost immediately upon emerging from the streambeds, sockeye have adapted to using the lake environment for spawning and rearing the juvenile stages. Sockeye smolts spend one to three years in fresh water lakes feeding on zooplankton before heading downstream to the ocean. The sockeye salmon has a non-anadromous form called the kokanee which lives its entire life in fresh water, reaches only one to two pounds average weight and spawns at the same time, and often in the same waters, as the sea-going form.

Chum salmon (also called dog, because of the large teeth they develop in fresh water or calico, because of their pink and green spawning colors) spend three to four years at sea and while they average about seven pounds, grow as large as 40 pounds. They are fall spawners. Sockeye spend one to four years in salt water, return to the rivers in the summer when they average about seven pounds and spawn in the early fall. Their rich, red flesh makes them highly desirable and they are the economic mainstay of the commercial salmon fleet.

Pinks (also known as humpbacks or humpies because of the distinctive dorsal hump the spawning males develop) are the smallest and most numerous of the salmons, weighing three to four pounds at maturity. They make up more than half of the number of fish caught by the commercial salmon fleet. They arrive in July and August after about eighteen months at sea, and spawn in late summer and early fall, so all adults are two year olds. Pinks normally have a two-year

Chapter One: The Life Cycle of the Pacific Salmon

cyclic pattern of abundance, with even and odd year stocks being genetically distinct. Some rivers have only an odd- or even-year run, and others have both, but one is usually dominant. Pink salmon adults spawn in fast-flowing, shallow riffles in substantial groups and their huge numbers represent a major source of nutrients to the riverine ecology.

All members of the Pacific salmon family are anadromous, meaning that they spend different lengths of time in fresh water, descend to the oceans to feed, and then return to fresh water to spawn. They all die after spawning with the exception of cutthroat trout, steelhead and its resident form, the rainbow trout. It was not until the 1970s that it became universally accepted that the salmon are able to identify through their sense of smell not only their natal rivers but also the very same gravel beds that gave them life. Salmon whose nostrils were plugged or nasal nerves were cut swam past their home waters, while those who were left in their natural state unerringly found their way home. How they can migrate thousands of miles out to the open ocean and return en masse to the same river is still a matter of speculation, however.

All Pacific salmon return to the rivers in large schools with each species returning to spawn together in specific areas of the watershed and at different times. Through this strategy, nature has reduced the likelihood of hybridization, the competition between the adults of the different

Spawning pink salmon.

Photographed by Fred Seiler

A school of pink salmon adults.

species for suitable spawning areas and the competition between the juveniles for food. At the same time, this pattern of behaviour ensures that the marine environment's nutrients will be transported throughout the entire river system, from the estuary to the headwaters.

It really pays for a trout angler to learn about the habits of the salmon in the rivers he fishes. Knowing when and where each species lays its eggs makes it easier to find the trout and char that wait behind the spawning salmon for the eggs that drift downstream. I have stood on the bank of a small Alaskan stream watching spawning chum salmon and have seen dozens of large Dolly Varden right in amongst them, waiting for a free meal. Under conditions such as these, trout can become quite selective to eggs, requiring imitations which match the natural in size, color and buoyancy.

Where the eggs are laid in fall, the fry will emerge in the spring. In the gravel beds below a lake near where I live, first the pinks, then the coho spawn in fall. In the spring, steelhead spawn in the same areas. Chinook and chum spawn in deeper waters downstream in late summer, and the sockeye spawn in the river above the lake in the early fall. I expect to see the fry appear in the same order and in the same places, so I know which imitations to be fishing when. Recognizing the different fry in the water also helps to ensure that I am using the correct fly, because trout, especially the larger ones, do become selective.

Finally, knowing where drifting salmon flesh is likely to wind up makes it more productive to fish flesh flies in the late-autumn months after the salmon have spawned and died. Each region and each watershed has its unique seasons of the salmon and nothing beats taking the time to become familiar with the special characteristics of the rivers you plan to fish.

Chapter One: The Life Cycle of the Pacific Salmon

CHAPTER TWO

Spring Time

The Features of Salmon Alevin, Fry and Smolts and Tying Flies to Imitate Them

For several weeks I had been visiting my favourite Skeena tributary, trekking through the shrinking snowdrifts that hung on in the forests that border the river. The days were becoming longer and warmer, and the buds on the trees promised that spring was imminent. I knew steelhead would be found in the riffles, some the dark fish that had arrived in the fall and wintered in the pools and nearby lake; others, far fewer, the bright fish of spring that had recently entered the river from the ocean. I enjoyed the thrill of the take as my bright fly was stopped in mid-drift and a strong steelhead rolled at the surface; I was satisfied to bring the fish into shore and to release it to fulfill its biological drive. But what I was really waiting for were the little

Salmon fry in hands.

darting, twinkling movements in the shallows and back eddies that announced the arrival of the true harbingers of spring—the newly emerged salmon fry.

Even in the cold, blustery days of late March, a few hardy fry could be found along the edges of shallow riffles, absorbing the warmth of the strengthening sun, but their numbers were not sufficient to draw the trout out of the nearby lake. Then one day, when the swallows dipped over the stream, feeding on the clouds of midges, and the trees fuzzed green with leaves, there they were, schools of darting coho fry in every slough and backwater. It is a truly magical phenomenon to witness: the silvery fry seem to bubble and boil out of the very gravel like an alchemist's dream of turning stone into precious metal. I have reached down and lifted up a handful of wet pebbles and watched fascinated as it came alive with twisting little fry that dropped through my fingers into the stream. Suddenly, where there was barren water, now there is life.

Within days, the river is full of trout, char, whitefish and squawfish, ravenous from a long winter, that have dropped down from the lake to feast on nature's bounty. This is the time the trout fisherman has been waiting for. For a few weeks in spring, the river holds more and larger fish than at any other time of the year, and when conditions are right it is the best chance an expert angler has of landing the fish of a lifetime. Large trout gorge themselves on the fry of the salmon: pinks, sockeye,

Chapter Two: Spring Time

coho, chum and chinook. It is among the best times to introduce a neophyte to the joys of fly-fishing because, at least during the early stages of the fry hatch, any clumsily cast silvery fly will take trout. It is truly "Duffer's Week."

But as the fry season progresses and the high, turbid waters of spring give way to lower, clearer flows, the trout, especially the larger ones, become warier and harder to fool. No longer will just any streamer take trout consistently. To be productive, the fly-fisher has to match the size, coloration and behaviour of the particular salmon juveniles which the trout are feeding on that day. A little careful observation and knowledge will pay off handsomely, if you can identify the juvenile salmonids and fish a close imitation.

Salmon and Steelhead Alevin, Fry and Smolt Features

The eggs of the various salmon species which were laid in the redds in late summer and early fall during cooling water temperatures, incubated in their gravel beds during the winter, and developed into alevin with the warming temperatures of spring. The young salmonids are referred to as alevin while they retain their yolk sacs, the remnant of the egg upon which they feed initially, and as fry after they have absorbed the sac. The time the eggs take to develop into alevins varies according to the temperature range they experience during incubation, but by roughly 5-8 months after spawning, most salmon eggs have hatched. Even under optimum natural conditions

Salmon fry bubbling out of the gravel.

only 10-20 percent of the eggs successfully develop into alevin, and the ratio can be as low as one percent.

The newly hatched alevin can move fairly extensively through the gravel and often stay under its surface until their yolk sac is almost completely absorbed. While in the gravel, the eggs and alevins are eaten by various predators such as sculpins, leeches and invertebrates. Many eggs do not hatch and many alevins do not successfully emerge from the gravel, so there is plenty of food for these predators to scavenge. They ultimately have a beneficial effect on the streambed ecology by removing the dead eggs and alevins, which by decomposing would have competed with next year's eggs for oxygen.

Water temperature and light conditions are the key factors in the timing of when fry emerge from the gravel. Referring to sockeye salmon, R.A. Bams said that "in nature, the daily light and temperature cycles cause fry migrants to accumulate just below the surface of gravel beds towards dusk when the water temperature is high. Upon nightfall the inhibitory action of the light is removed, and the migrants enter the open water. In a matter of hours, most of the accumulated fish have emerged, the daily run is past its peak, and the numbers drop off to a low level. These latter fish are those that have only just reached the surface of the gravel. Towards dawn the water temperature is low, fish activity drops, and light will again inhibit any further emergence."

Biologists speculate that this phototropic (light-avoiding) behaviour is an adaptation to reduce the predation of trout and other fishes on the newly emerged fry. It certainly goes a long way to explaining why the peak of trout activity frequently occurs during the hour or so just before and after dark in the evening and just after sunrise in the morning.

The timing of this predator/prey relationship is evident on many rivers where salmon fry are part of the spring feast for trout. Each spring for the last nine years, I have made the trip to Rainbow Alley, the short section of the Babine River which connects the west arm of Babine Lake to Nilkitkwa Lake, really just a widening of the river itself. Large rainbow trout and char enter the river to feed on the millions of sockeye fry and smolts that migrate up and down the river in the late spring. The lake is 3000 feet up in the mountains, so even during a normal year spring comes two to three weeks later than in the valley. When spring has been late and water temperatures have been cooler than normal, we have arrived too early for the peak of the sockeye fry hatch on the Babine, even though the fry have come and gone in the rivers in the valleys below.

Several studies of Babine Lake sockeye over the years have estimated that of the 3200 average number of eggs a typical female lays, 80% are lost during spawning, incubation, emergence and migration to the lake, resulting in 640 fry. During their lake residency, 90% of these fry are lost to predators, resulting in 64 smolts that head downriver to live in the ocean. Again, 90% of these are lost, which leaves two adults to return to spawn, maintaining a stable population. (Johnson, quoted in Levy and Hall) Other studies have put the total mortality rate between

Rainbow Alley.

63% and 87%, but no matter what the correct rate is, it's obvious that the juvenile salmon are a major source of food for predators in fresh water.

Although it is possible to catch fish all day long when the fry are drifting through downriver, especially on overcast and dark days, the river really seems to come alive in the early morning and late evening. By early June at this latitude the nights are very short, so we're talking about getting up at four in the morning to fish and staying up to eleven or later in the evening. The only way to survive this brutal regime is to take a long, mid-afternoon siesta!

At the alevin stage, all salmon juveniles look very similar regardless of species, so there is little point in tying anything but a general imitation. Their bodies are long, thin and translucent with a darker lateral line. The eye is relatively large and dominant and the egg sac, which constitutes about 60% of the body weight, hangs, red-orange and translucent, from their bellies. There is considerable variation in the amount of yolk material which remains unused at the time the fry emerge from the gravel and the reasons for this are not clear. Biologists speculate, for example, that sockeye fry which have to travel greater distances to the nursery lakes retain a greater portion of their yolk sacs to provide energy for this journey. This is a characteristic of the sockeye fry on the Babine River, for instance, since many of them have a large sac for several days after emergence and show a red stripe in the belly for awhile longer.

Modern alevin patterns.

Traditional Alevin Patterns

One of the most successful traditional patterns for imitating the newly emerged alevin struggling along the gravel bottom of the stream is the venerable Egg 'n' I, Alevin or Yolk Sac. British Columbia angler, Tommy Brayshaw, developed it in 1939 to imitate the sockeye fry of the Little and Adams rivers. The original was basically a variation of the old standard English sea-trout fly, the Mallard and Silver, with a silver tinsel body, a light mallard flank wing and a throat "hackle" of red Indian crow feather. Although over the years, Brayshaw also used white polar bear hair for the wing, the Egg 'n' I which is tied today is very similar to the original except that red wool or polypropylene are substituted for Indian crow. The Egg 'n' I is easy to tie and should be in every trout fisherman's fly box for those times when salmon fry have just popped out of the gravel.

Egg 'N' I

Chapter Two: Spring Time

Egg 'n' I and Rolled Muddler.

Egg 'N' I

HOOK: Traditionally, a #6 or #8 low-water salmon hook, but usually now a #10 or #12 3X long streamer hook such as the Mustad 9671
THREAD: Black 6/0
BODY: Flat silver tinsel
THROAT: Red-orange wool or polypropylene fibers
WING: Strips or rolled light mallard flank, sometimes tied down at tail

Whereas the Egg 'n' I was developed in the interior of British Columbia to imitate specifically newly emerged sockeye fry, another pattern developed for a completely different purpose has proven also to be a very effective imitation of salmon fry, especially when they are in the surface film of streams and rivers. The Rolled Muddler with its wing and tail of rolled light mallard flank fibers, which gave it its name, was originated in the 1970s by Tom Murray as an imitation of sticklebacks for sea-run cutthroats; a purpose for which it proved most effective. Once other anglers learned of Murray's version of the original Muddler Minnow, they began using it throughout the province and today you would be hard pressed to find a trout fisherman who does not use the Rolled Muddler as one of his mainstays during the spring salmon hatch. I think the red thread which is tied to show at the throat and head of the fly is suggestive of the remains of the egg sac which persists as a red stripe on sockeye fry for several days or weeks after the egg sac has been absorbed. There are several popular variations of Murray's silver-bodied original. A common one uses gold tinsel and tan-dyed mallard fibers for a duller pattern to use in low-water, bright light conditions. Others use dark green, olive-brown or dark-brown dyed mallard for more accurate imitations of the various salmon fry.

Rolled Muddler

HOOK: #10 or #12 3X long-streamer such as Mustad 9671
THREAD: Red 6/0
TRAIL: Light mallard flank fibers about as long as the body
BODY: Medium flat silver tinsel, ribbed with medium oval silver tinsel, wound in reverse
WING: Rolled strips of light mallard flank fibers or other dyed mallard it is very common to include a few strands of pearlescent or silver Crystal Hair under the mallard wing.)
HEAD: Light deer hair spun on as a mallard head with a few strands of deer hair over the body. (Do not tie a large, tightly packed head as you would for most Muddler Minnows, because you want the Rolled Muddler to fish in the surface film.)
THROAT: Tie red thread so that some shows at the throat of the fly to suggest the remnants of the egg sac. Darker Variation

As above, but with tan-colored (wood duck) dyed mallard flank fibers for tail and wing, gold tinsel for the body, and tan-colored deer hair for the head.

Three Modern Alevin Patterns

Hugh Storey's Albino Alevin

This unique pattern is based on Hugh Storey's observations at the local fish hatchery in Kitimat, British Columbia, where he lives. Some years the hatchery produces large numbers of albino chinook salmon fry and they stand out noticeably among their darker siblings.

"An albino fry can't hide so he's going to get eaten right away in the wild," Storey said. A self-taught fly-tier, he decided to create a pattern that would stand out just like the albino naturals he saw in the hatchery. The result was his Albino Alevin.

"I use it in the spring for trout and on coastal rivers for steelhead. It really produces on the Stellako River, and when it does, I hardly bother with anything else."

HOOK: #6 or #8 Tiemco 2457 scud or caddis hook
THREAD: Clear monofilament
TAIL: Fine, silver Flashabou
BODY: A plastic tube-fly liner
EGG SAC: Red-orange yarn tied underneath
EYES: Pearlescent 2 mm stick-on eyes covered in head cement

TYING INSTRUCTIONS

Step 1: Tie a base of clear monofilament thread onto the hook.
Step 2: Weight with around fifteen wraps of fine lead wire.
Step 3: Cut the tube-fly liner into 3/4" section.
Step 4: Grab about 8-10 strands of fine, silver Flashabou and one strand of peacock herl (to imitate the lateral line) and thread them into the tube with a line threader.
Step 5: Pull them out the end of the tube. Trim off to make a tail and fill the tube, leaving Flashabou long in front of the tube.
Step 6: Take tube to the end of the lead and tie in, first the strands of Flashabou and

Spring on a Skeena tributary.

then the plastic tube body, leaving half of the tube for the body.

Step 7: Fold the Flashabou back along the top of the hook and tie back to the end of the lead to make a dorsal fin.

Step 8: Flip the hook over and tie in an egg sac underneath the body, using bright red-orange yarn or pale pink chenille.

Step 9: Stick on a pair of pearlescent, sticky 2mm eyes and cover head with a light coating of cement or epoxy.

Blane Chocklett's "Gummy Minnow" Alevin

The first time I saw Blane Chocklett's alevin pattern I was stunned by how life-like it was. The soft, flexible body material made it look and feel as if I were holding a fresh, wet juvenile salmon in my hands. The transparent, pearly body and orange egg sac glowed in the light and I half-expected the darn thing to move!

The secret to the realism of Chocklett's imitation is a new material he and friend Harrison R. Steeves developed called Sili-Skin, a sheet of silicone rubber with a colored foil underlay and adhesive back. The owner of Blue Ridge Fly-fishers in Virginia, Chocklett first used the material to make a saltwater baitfish imitation he called the Gummy Minnow and which has proven itself as a really productive fly for false albacore. Then he began experimenting with everything from squid to sand-eel imitations. Finally, he tried his hand at the salmon alevin and the result wound up in my hand on that memorable day. Umpqua Feather Merchants is carrying Chocklett's Gummy Minnow.

Preparing the Material for the Gummy Minnow Alevin

Sili-Skin comes in 2" x 6" sheets and is a tricky material to work with because of its adhesive backing, so be careful when handling it not to let the sticky side touch itself. Likewise, avoid stretching the material when applying it to the hook because if one side is stretched more than the other, when they are joined together, the body will curl in that direction.

TYING INSTRUCTIONS

Step 1: Begin by cutting the belly color (mother of pearl for the alevin) from the sheet of Sili-Skin in a 2" x 1" strip.

Step 2: Next, cut the strip lengthwise in the middle, leaving a small section the length of the hook shank uncut.

Step 3: Now, prepare a thin section of Sili-Skin in the back color (Road Slick) about 1/8 inch thick and 2 inches long.

Step 4: Lastly, prepare another strip of mother of pearl Sili-Skin about 2" x 2" for the final covering.

TYING INSTRUCTIONS

Step 1: Wrap a short-shank straight-eyed hook with a base of white thread and tie off. Then wrap the shank with fine silver wire to hold a short section of thick fluorescent red thread in place. Pull the thread out of the way and hold in place with a clip on the vise.

Step 2: Take the mother of pearl strip you partially cut and peel the backing off. Be careful not to let the sticky sides touch. Position the piece so that the split end is facing towards the rear of the hook. Pull the two split tails apart slightly and bring the uncut portion up to the bottom of the hook. Pull the red thread down below the hook shank before folding the two sections of Sili-Skin together. Be careful not to stretch either one.

Step 3: Next cut the top portion at an angle from the hook eye to the tail.

Step 4: Then cut from the back corner to the bend of the hook at a downward angle to complete the shape of the alevin.

Step 5: Take the 1/8 " x 2" strip of Road Slick Sili-Skin and pull the backing off. Center and lay the strip over the back and fold down evenly on each side. Then trim the outline of the belly.

Step 6: Place sticky 2mm pearlescent eyes on each side of the head.

Step 7: Tie in the thread at the hook eye. Run a fluorescent red bead on the red thread and tie off at the head so that the bead is snug against the hook shank.

Step 8: Take the larger piece of mother of pearl skin and pull the backing off. Center and lay the strip over the back and fold down evenly over each side, making sure to encase the bead. Trim the outline of the belly to include the bead egg sac.

Step 9: Reattach the thread and tied down the Sili-Skin with strong wraps. Tear off and trim any excess protruding past the hook eye and whip finish.

David Sloan's American Alevin (Pink and Orange)

David Sloan is an innovative fly tier working for the American Fly-fishing Company in Sacramento, California, and his experiments have led to a unique alevin pattern which Umpqua will be selling too. Sloan makes use of the crochet weave technique to produce a durable and effective fly. It is a little complicated to tie, but the result is worth the effort. The parr marks show through the clear vinyl rib and the wing of fine fibers adds movement and life to the imitation.

HOOK:	TMC 2302, size 8 and 10
THREAD:	White or gray 6/0
TAIL:	Pearl Wing 'N' Flash (or substitute like Angel Hair)
BODY:	Clear small vinyl rib using the crochet weave
BELLY:	Pearl Wing 'N' Flash (or substitute like Angel Hair)
EGG SAC:	Fluorescent Hot Pink or Orange Diamond Braid
UNDER WING:	Pearl Wing 'N' Flash (or substitute like Angel Hair)
OVER WING:	Gray Kinkyfiber
EYES:	5/32-inch 3-D molded eyes
HEAD:	Epoxied

TYING INSTRUCTIONS

Step 1: Tie in a base of white thread from the eye of the hook back to about the width of the gap of the hook.

Step 2: Take about 30 fibers of Pearl Wing 'N' Flash and tie them in, facing backwards, where the thread was stopped. Continue wrapping the thread over the fibers to the bend of the hook, keeping the fibers on top of the hook. Advance the thread to the eye of the hook. The tail should be about 1 1/2 times the length of the body and have a ragged edge, rather than an abrupt one.

Step 3: Tie one piece of clear vinyl rib on top of the hook and one underneath, both facing towards the tail.

Step 4: Form an even underbody with the white thread and advance the thread to the original tie-in point.

Step 5: Using the gray thread, form three distinct, evenly-spaced parr marks about 1/16 inch wide. Begin the first parr mark about 1/16 inch from the tail end of the body. Whip finish. Repeat 1/2 way towards the head and at a point equal to the distance between the other two.

Step 6: Rotate the hook sideways and weave the vinyl rib forwards using the crochet weave technique described on pages 202 and 203 in *The Fly Tier's Benchside Reference* by Ted Leeson and Jim Schollmeyer. Continue weaving the body to a point about a hook gap away from the eye of the hook. Reattach the white thread and tie off the vinyl rib, keeping the tag end of the top part on top of the hook and the tag end of the bottom part on the bottom of the hook.

Step 7: Tie in a small amount of Pearl Wing 'N' Flash (or substitute like Angel Hair) on the bottom of the hook where the vinyl rib was tied off. It should extend about 1/8" beyond the tail. Trim with scissors to create a tapered belly.

Step 8: Tie in a loop of fluorescent hot pink or orange Diamond Braid on the bottom of the hook where the Pearl Wing 'N' Flash was tied in. The egg sac should be slightly smaller than the head.

Step 9: Tie in another small amount of Pearl Wing 'N' Flash on top of the hook and repeat process #7.

Step 10: Tie in 5-8 fibers of Kinkyfiber on top of the hook, about 1/8 inch longer than the tail and taper it too.

Step 11: Build a tapered head with the thread and whip finish.

Step 12: Place a 5/32-inch 3-D molded eye on each side of the head.

Step 13: Using epoxy cement, form a tapered head that covers the entire head of the fly.

The Characteristics of the Various Salmon Fry and Smolts

Pink and chum fry.

Photographed by Fred Seiler

Once they have lost their egg sacs, salmon juveniles are called fry. In the case of pink and chum salmon, these fry migrate downstream immediately to the ocean and are thus available to trout for several weeks only. Sockeye fry first drift downstream individually, usually under the cover of darkness, and then frequently migrate upstream in schools to the nursery lake, mostly during daylight hours. For example, sockeye fry in the Babine system will drift down Rainbow Alley into Nilkitkwa Lake and then turn around later and ascend the river back into Babine Lake where they will stay for one to two years. Combined with the downstream migration of sockeye smolts which occurs at the same time, these movements provide a major feeding opportunity for trout in the river. The length of time that chinook fry rear in fresh water is variable, with some southern populations staying for three months or less, and northern populations staying up to a year. The majority of coho fry that emerge remain in the stream for one to two years and are the most commonly seen fry along the margins of streams and rivers. As a result, they are subject to heavy predation by trout, char, other fishes and birds. The fry of the anadromous form of *Oncorhynchus mykiss*, the steelhead, rear in fresh water for up to three years, and can be found spread throughout a river system, even into the lakes. For the angler, being familiar with the behaviour and appearances of the various salmon fry is the key to finding and using fly patterns that will be accepted by the trout.

Pink and Chum Salmon Fry

Pink fry

In late March, my friend, Fred Seiler, a fishing guide and ecotourism operator in the Skeena area, was exploring a tributary when he noticed a kingfisher sitting on a gravel bar, apparently digging a hole. Seiler said, "I don't know how the kingfisher knew there were fry in the hole, but when I went over, I saw that it was filled with fry."

Pink and chum fry were stacked up with their heads popping out of the gravel and their gills barely in the little water that was in the hole. Seiler lifted several rocks and under each he found dozens more fry in the same vertical position. "I realized that the whole gravel bed we were walking on must have been alive with salmon fry," he said. He spent the next half hour filling his hat with fry and transporting them to the river.

Chapter Two: Spring Time

Chum fry

What Seiler found is typical of salmon fry ready to emerge in the spring. The alevins emerge from the eggs after an incubation of 3-5 months and stay in the gravel until they have completely absorbed the egg sac. They are able to move through the gravel where the adults laid their eggs in the previous fall, and they swim upwards through the crevices into the stream flow. They then head to the surface to take several gulps of air to fill their swim bladder and achieve neutral density. After emergence, pink and chum salmon fry migrate quickly downstream to salt water, usually between mid-April and mid-May. Although they are not available in the rivers for very long, their huge numbers and strong tendency to school mean that in certain waters, the trout do have the opportunity to feed on them extensively.

The amount of pink and chum fry that emerge is astonishing. One Easter weekend when Seiler and I were wading a small coastal river in the Northwest, we came across a school of several thousand chum fry in a small backwater, just waiting for the cover of darkness to travel the short distance downstream to salt water. The bottom of the shallow side channel was black with a moving

Chum fry.

mass of literally thousands of chum fry. Later that day, we caught a half dozen good-sized Dolly Varden on matching fry patterns, evidence that these predators were gorging themselves on this springtime feast.

Although pink and chum fry in coastal rivers wait until dark to descend to the ocean to reduce the chances of being eaten, in large inland rivers like the Skeena the fry are more likely to migrate during daylight hours because of the distance to the ocean. When they do, the predation rates are extremely high. Biologists have estimated that in certain rivers up to 90% of the fry are consumed by char, salmon smolts and trout on the way downstream.

Pink salmon fry are very easy to recognize in the water: they are slender in shape with very silvery sides, no parr marks, a shiny dark-green back, and are about 30-35 mm long. I frequently first see small schools of pink fry wiggling in the slower current behind rocks. Over the years, I have noticed that Dolly Varden char in particular seem to target the pink fry and will venture into the shallow edges of the stream to ambush the hapless juveniles as they emerge and drift downstream. When char or trout are feeding on pink fry in these situations, there is

School of chum fry.

no mistaking the activity because their slashing attacks are often startlingly explosive. For the several weeks in which the schools of pink fry are migrating towards the ocean, the river is full of large char of a size you would only catch in lakes at any other time of the year.

The newly hatched fry have to run a gauntlet of cutthroat trout and char that enter these rivers to feed on them, but even when they have made it to the brackish estuary waters, the large schools of pink and chum fry have no sanctuary. Because of their schooling instinct, pink fry will move in large numbers along the shoreline, milling about in bays for days and even weeks, before heading out into the ocean. In the bright sunlight, you can see long, undulating strands of countless fry following the coastline past kelp beds and boat docks. Sea-run cutthroats will drop back into the estuaries with the fry and continue to feed on them. If you hit the right time, usually during or just after high tide, you can have some exciting fly-fishing for cutties in brackish water from beaches or from a belly boat in quiet bays.

Sockeye Fry and Smolts

Sockeye fry.

Unlike pink and chum fry, sockeye fry stay in fresh water after emerging, living in a lake for one or two years before heading back to sea as smolts. Trout fishing in the river systems where sockeye spawn is some of the best available, especially in the sections of rivers below the lakes where the fry and smolts rear. For example, Babine Lake is the primary

Sockeye fry

nursery for sockeye in the Skeena River system and the huge numbers of naturally spawned fry are supplemented by those released from the Fulton River and Pinkut Creek spawning channels. Where the lake flows into the river at Fort Babine, Rainbow Alley funnels millions of fry and smolts into a narrow channel at the outlet. Similar situations exist on the Stellako, Chilko, Horsefly, Harrison, Adams and other river systems in British Columbia that have nursery lakes for sockeye.

The lakes act as natural filters and rarely is the water below these outlets discolored by rains, runoff or glacial silt. The steady flows, clear waters and rich food sources attract large hungry trout from out of the lakes to feed on the emerging fry and the migrating smolts in the spring. The decomposing corpses of the adults continue to enrich these waters all year long, supporting incredibly dense populations of caddis, mayflies and stoneflies, and adding to food chain that grows large trout. Then, in the fall, the sockeye eggs provide even more protein to these rivers.

The effect of this redistribution of marine nutrients to the fresh water ecosystem is to create a remarkable abundance of animal and plant life. The upper Babine River from Fort Babine to where it empties into Nilkitkwa Lake at the end of the four-mile-long Rainbow Alley is a perfect example. Ringed by rugged, snow-capped peaks for much of the year, the river banks and estuary are home to an incredible array of shorebirds, waterfowl and wildlife. Ospreys, bald eagles, mergansers, western grebes, gulls and kingfishers nest near the river and feed their young on the various stages of the sockeye's lifecycle. Bears grow fat on the salmon and the grasses that the decaying fish fertilize with their bodies. The thick willow swamps and hardwood forests abound with moose, and the river and lake support otters and mink that feed on juvenile and adult salmon. Humans too have lived along the river for thousands of years, relying on the runs of salmon for food. Smokehouse Island is so named because this is where the Wetsuweten First Nations that live at Fort Babine each year net and smoke the rich, orange flesh of the sockeye salmon to prepare their food for the winter.

Chapter Two: Spring Time

Although sockeye eggs are most commonly laid in redds in tributaries adjacent to the rearing lakes such as the Babine, in some areas sockeye spawn along lakeshores where spring water up wells. Spawning occurs in late summer and early fall and the eggs have the longest incubation period of any of the Pacific salmon—up to 300 days, but averaging about 150 in most of British Columbia. In most cases, sockeye fry also use up their yolk sac the most quickly of any salmon, although there are a few exceptions, like the Babine sockeye mentioned earlier.

Sockeye fry are about 30 mm long when they emerge from the gravel and when they have lost their egg sac, they are an iridescent olive-brown above the lateral line, with mother-of-pearl sides and a white belly. They exhibit a dozen or so irregular parr marks whose length is

Sockeye smolts.

less than the vertical diameter of the eye and that extend below the lateral line. As with all fry, the red of the gills shows distinctly through the semi-transparent gill covers. They can be easily distinguished from chum fry which have larger fins, larger, irregular parr marks, and green coloring on their backs which does not extend as far down the sides.

The main period of emergence seems to be at night, so that is why early morning and late evening are the most productive times to fish for trout at this time of year. The sockeye fry will emerge from the gravel beds throughout the river and will be swept downstream. It is easy to know when sockeye fry are moving. On the Babine, Bonaparte gulls

Chapter Two: Spring Time

swoop and dive at individual schools of sockeye as they drift downstream and feeding trout betray their presence by repeatedly porpoising after the migrants, like U-boats attacking Atlantic convoys. Oftentimes on the Babine River, I have seen the water surface dimpling with the movements of thousands of fry drifting in the currents. At times like this, every trout in the river begins to feed, and just as quickly stops when the schools have passed by.

Although the alevin emerge in the middle of the river and mostly at night, during the day, many of the sockeye fry swim back upstream along the banks of the river back into the nursery lake. Schools of a hundred or more swirl along the banks of the river hiding on the edge of the reeds, little pale ghosts, easily seen in the clear water if you know where to look for them. Trout will continue all day to pick them off in the little side channels as they migrate upstream. It is not unusual to have a greedy trout whose belly is distended with dozens of fry disgorge a half a dozen freshly ingested little sockeye, some of them still alive.

As if this smorgasbord of fry were not enough food for the hungry trout, the downstream emergence of sockeye smolts coincides with the emergence and migrations of their younger relatives. The fry have stayed in the rearing lakes for one to two years, growing up to 100 mm in length and weighing from 5-10 grams. When the smolts are travelling across the North Arm of Babine Lake prior to entering the river, the lake's surface looks as if rain is falling, there are so many smolts swirling just below the surface. Now and then, several smolts leap free of the surface, flashing silver in the sunlight, evidence that the large rainbows and charr that congregate where the lake narrows into the river are feeding on them. Balls of smolts, some containing thousands of individuals, float by under my anchored boat, their silvery heads repeatedly breaking the surface as the school continues on its journey to the ocean hundreds of miles away. A few large smolts can make quite a mouthful for a trout.

I remember one occasion on the Babine when I decided to kill a good-sized trout for supper, a rare and relished occurrence. When I cleaned the fish, I discovered it had six large sockeye smolts in its stomach, the largest being about the length and thickness of my thumb, so I immediately began fishing with a larger streamer pattern to good effect.

Coho Fry and Smolts

Coho fry are the ones most commonly seen along the stream margins and they are present all year long, so they are a constant food source to trout. Although their numbers suggest they are schooling, in fact coho fry do not really react as a school, but instead exhibit individual behaviour. They are readily recognizable in the water and hard to confuse with any other fry because their tail, ventral and pectoral fins are distinctively orange. As fry, they are 30-50 mm in length, darker in color than other fry, with an olive-brown back and almost bronze

Coho fry

sides. They have a white belly and large regular parr marks extending below the lateral line.

It takes about 50 days on average for coho eggs to hatch and the fry, about 30mm in length, emerge from the gravel about three weeks later. Unlike most other fry, coho will frequently stay close to the site where they emerged, sheltering in quiet backwaters, side channels and swampy areas, although some fry will rear in lakes. They especially like to hide in feeder creeks where there is cover such as overhanging branches. There are several marshy areas adjacent to my favorite Skeena tributary and each spring, as the skunk cabbage shoots emerge, I look out for the first signs of coho fry in the little muddy trickles that run through the swamp. The coho fry flush into the main stream during a spring freshet and will stay in fresh water for one to three years, reaching a size of 100-150 mm and a weight of 10-25 grams before dropping down to the estuary.

More than any other salmon,

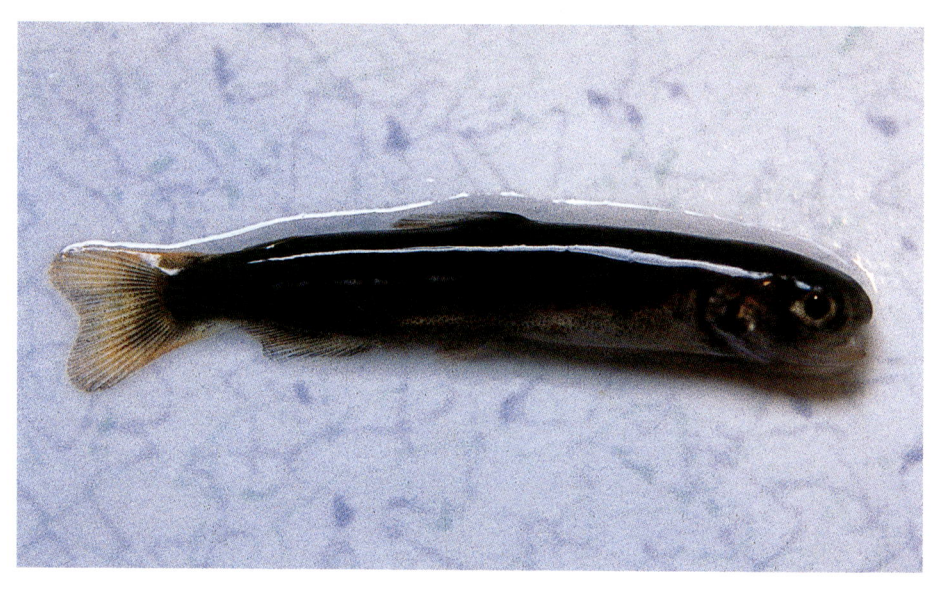

Coho fry.

Chapter Two: Spring Time

coho will utilize the marshy areas of a river drainage, even the beaver ponds. I remember fly-fishing one fall in a large beaver pond behind where I was living on the Kispiox and unexpectedly catching a chunky little coho smolt of about six inches on a dry fly, not much smaller than the small cutthroat trout that lived there. When trout are feeding on coho fry and smolts, small Muddlers and other darker streamers are good patterns to imitate them.

Chinook Fry

The remnants of snow drifts still remained in the forests along the Kitimat River when I ventured out on my first fly-fishing expedition of the year. Here and there pussy willows and catkins suggested the beginnings of spring, and occasionally the sun broke through the scudding, gray clouds, but the cold, damp gusts from nearby Douglas Channel left no doubt that winter had not yet relinquished its hold. As I splashed upstream through the shallows of a short rapid section of the river, I was surprised to see large, dark fry furrowing the water as they fled my clumsy advance. Chinook fry, I thought. Let's see if the sea-run cutties will take a fly. A little while later, in a deep pool at the mouth of a tributary stream, my suspicions were confirmed when I landed four strong trout that had obviously been feeding on the newly emerged fry, the largest a beautifully coloured 3 1/2 pounder.

Chinook lay their eggs in the gravel in the deep, faster runs of larger rivers and therefore, their fry emerge in these areas. Flooding is a major cause of egg losses in all species and it is estimated that less than 40 percent of the chinook eggs laid in a redd make it to the fry stage. In fine gravel, over 80 percent of the emerged alevin never make it to the water surface, compared to a 80-90 percent success rate in coarser gravel.

Some chinook fry migrate quickly downstream to the estuary and others stay in the stream for up to a year or more. Why there is this difference no one knows for sure, but some suggest heavier flows displace the fry downstream, or that the estuaries are simply the preferred rearing areas for some of the stock. In any case, chinook fry are the largest upon emergence and continue to grow faster, from .33 mm a day to .86 mm a day, so they make a tempting mouthful

Chinook fry.

Cannibal Trout

for trout while they are in fresh water. Because sockeye, coho, chinook and steelhead fry stay in fresh water for varying lengths of time, the angler should carry patterns in a variety of sizes to match the growing fry throughout the summer.

Traditional Salmon Fry Imitations: Haig-Brown's Fry Patterns

British Columbia's dean of fly-fishers, Roderick Haig-Brown, realized early in his years in the province that tying accurate imitations of the salmon fry was critical to success in catching trout in the spring. He disliked the tied-down wing patterns that were commonly used because he thought they looked stiff and dead, and preferred instead flies that used loose feathers and hair, especially polar bear, because they looked more life-like and flexible. He said, "... I believe that size is important, and shape, and anything that contributes to the impression of swift life that is a small fish."

His observations hold as true today: cutthroat and rainbow trout can become very selective to color, size, shape and movement when they are feeding on salmon fry. Haig-Brown tied flies that imitated each of the salmon fry and experimented with retrieves that would present the flies to the feeding trout in as natural a manner as possible.

He tied his series of fry imitations on a low-water Atlantic salmon hook, convinced of its superiority over the long-shanked streamer hook. Haig-Brown said he experimented every year with new fry patterns, but eventually he settled on four patterns: the Silver Brown, a coho and cutthroat trout fry imitation; Silver Lady, a chinook and chum fry imitation; the Humpback Fry; and the General Fry Imitation.

The Silver Brown

This pattern effectively imitates the dark-bronze of the coho fry's sides, the mottled parr marks and the orange tail and fins. As with all his fry patterns, Haig-Brown tied the Silver Brown on low-water japanned Atlantic salmon hooks, but with the incredible array of excellent hooks available today, his flies can be tied just as effectively on lighter modern wet-fly hooks.

HOOK:	#6 or #8, low-water Atlantic salmon hook
THREAD:	Black 6/0
TAIL:	A small, red-orange Indian crow feather, or substitute
BODY:	Flat silver tinsel
WING:	Orange polar bear underneath two slender strips of mottled golden pheasant-tail feather
HACKLE:	Natural red-brown hackle tied underneath

Chapter Two: Spring Time

Silver Lady

The teal strips of this pattern are very suggestive of the prominent parr marks on the chinook and chum frys' flanks.

HOOK:	#6 or larger, low-water Atlantic salmon hook
THREAD:	Black 6/0
TAIL:	A small, orange golden pheasant tippet
BODY:	Flat silver tinsel
WING:	Two silver badger hackles back to back; slender strips of teal on each side; four strands of peacock herl over the hackles; and a golden pheasant topping overall
HACKLE:	Badger hackle fibers tied underneath
CHEEKS:	Blue chatterer or kingfisher substitute

Humpback Fry Imitation

The dark, iridescent green of the peacock sword fibers imitate the shiny back of the pink fry perfectly and the silver tinsel is an essential component of good imitation.

HOOK:	#8, low-water Atlantic salmon hook
THREAD:	Black 6/0
TAIL:	Yellow hackle fibers
BODY:	Flat silver tinsel
WING:	Mixed green and blue polar bear hair with four or five peacock sword fibers overall
HACKLE:	Yellow hackle fibers

General Fry Imitation

Haig-Brown began fishing this pattern predominantly because it is an impressionistic pattern that can be taken by trout when any of the salmon, trout or stickleback fry are present.

HOOK:	#4 or #6, low-water Atlantic salmon hook
THREAD:	Black 6/0
TAIL:	A small, whole red feather
BODY:	Flat silver tinsel
WING:	A mix of green, yellow, blue, orange and some natural polar bear hair
HACKLE:	Red hackle fibers tied underneath

CHAPTER THREE

Fishing Salmon Alevin

Fry and Smolt "Hatches"

In the early part of the season, many of the traditional fry patterns, such as the Rolled Muddler, Egg 'n' I, and Mallard and Silver, are effective, as is the wet-fly technique of quartering downstream. As the season, progresses, however, trout—especially the larger ones—become warier in heavily-fished streams. That is the time to experiment with more realistic fly patterns and innovative casting techniques.

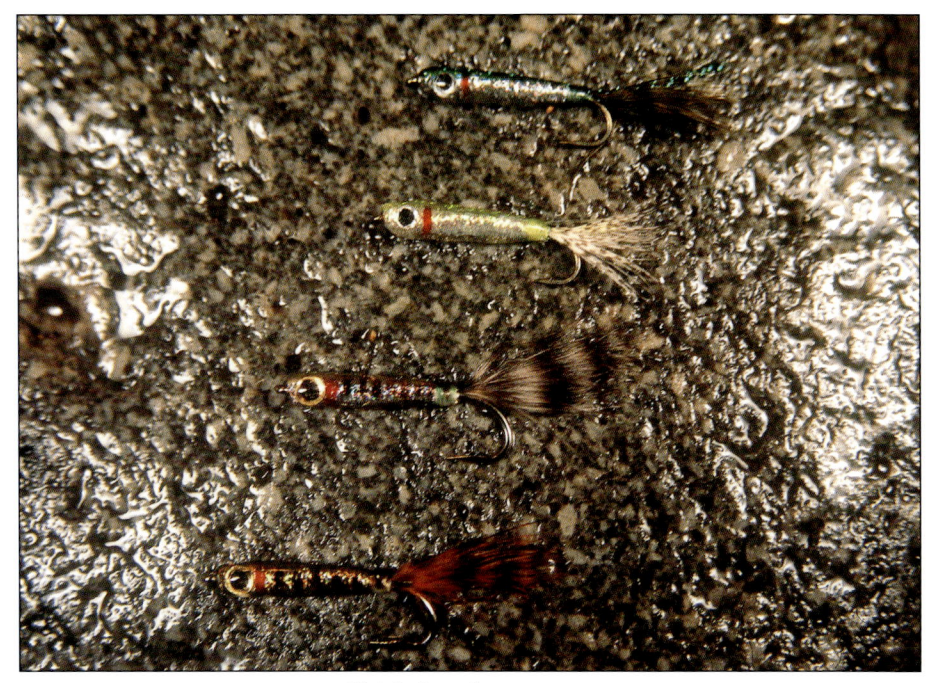

Chickabou fry patterns.

Chapter Three: Fishing Salmon Alevin 41

In recent years anglers have been toying with different materials and coming up with flies that match more and more closely the size, color and shape of the various salmon alevin, fry and smolts. Modern materials like fine Mylar tinsel can be used for wings and bodies; hot glue, epoxy, and silicon in liquid or sheets have been used to create egg sacs and translucent bodies; and marabou and synthetic hair have been used to create action in the flies. These experiments are continuing, but I have included some of the most recent and effective ones.

Coho chickabou fry.

Chickabou Fry

Watching salmon fry drifting in the surface film, I realized I needed a more accurate imitation of their appearance and movements. That's how the Chickabou Fry pattern was developed. I varied the colors of the slim, epoxy-coated body with its big eyes, slim silhouette to match the distinctive appearance of each of the different salmon fry. A tail of green, grizzly or orange chickabou, gave the fly the wiggle of the hapless fry drifting downstream and imitated the colors of pink, sockeye, and coho fry, respectively.

Sockeye chickabou fry (above) and Pink chickabou fry (below).

Chapter Three: Fishing Salmon Alevin

Chinook chickabou fry.

Chickabou Fry

HOOK: Tiemco 300, sizes #10 for sockeye, #8 for coho and pinks, #6 for chums and chinook
THREAD: White 6/0 or clear monofilament
EYES: 1.5 or 2mm prismatic stick-on eyes
BODY: Gudebrod Electra Braid holographic rod wrap in pearlescent (sockeye, chinook and chum); gold (coho); silver (humpback)
BACK: Neer Hair or similar synthetic hair with few strands of matching Crystal Hair: olive (sockeye, chinook and chum); brown (coho); dark green (humpback)
BELLY: White Neer Hair
TAIL: A few strands of pearlescent Crystal Hair and a chickabou feather: grizzly (sockeye, chinook and chum); orange (coho); green (humpback)

TYING INSTRUCTIONS

Step 1: Tie in the Crystal Hair and chickabou feather at tail first.
Step 2: Tie in Crystal Hair and Neer Hair for back and belly, with hair facing forward.
Step 3: Tie in Electra Braid.
Step 4: Wind thread back to tail. Wind Electra Braid to tail and tie in.
Step 5: Place eyes in place.
Step 6: Tie on red thread behind eyes.
Step 7: Bring back white belly hair and tie off with red thread.

Step 8: Bring back darker back hair and tie off with white thread at tail.
Step 9: Lightly coat body with 5-minute epoxy from head to tail.
Step 10: Put on a rotator to spread the epoxy evenly as it hardens. Don't touch for at least 3 hours.
Step 11: Parr marks can be added to the fry patterns (except for pinks) with a brown or black Pantone permanent marker.

A word about tying epoxy minnows: One weekend my fishing partner, Len Vanderstar, hooked seven good-sized trout in a row on the Babine with an epoxy minnow he had tied and was able to land only two fish. An inspection of his fly revealed that he had tied it too thick and had narrowed the hook gap so much that the fly was not penetrating enough to hold the trout. He trimmed the rear of the minnow body to a more tapered shape, thus widening the gap, and subsequently did not lose another fish.

Thunder Creek Sockeye Smolt

I first fished Keith Fulsher's Thunder Creek Baitfish flies in Eastern trout streams for brook trout and brown trout. Fulsher's series of flies imitated the predominant minnows and trout juveniles that were the diet of larger trout. His unique way of using bucktail for the head and wing provided a life-like silhouette and action to these successful flies. When I was looking for a pattern with which to imitate the sockeye fry that large trout fed on in Western rivers, I naturally turned to the Thunder Creek series for my inspiration because of their impressive success back East.

Thunder Creek Sockeye Smolt

HOOK:	Tiemco 300, #6 nickel-plated, ring-eyed streamer hook
THREAD:	White 6/0
HEAD:	Bucktail folded back and tied down, coated in epoxy
EYES:	1.5 or 2mm prismatic stick-on eyes
BODY:	White wool
RIBBING:	Medium embossed silver tinsel
WING:	An underling of two soft, webby grizzly saddle hackles, back to back. An overawing of olive-brown bucktail fibers and a few strands of pearlescent Crystal Flash
BELLY:	White bucktail fibers and a few strands of pearlescent Crystal Flash
TAIL:	Grizzly chickabou feather

Chapter Three: Fishing Salmon Alevin

TYING INSTRUCTIONS

Step 1: Cover shank of hook with white thread and return to point parallel with the barb.

Step 2: Tie in chickabou feather.

Step 3: Tie in medium embossed tinsel.

Step 4: Tie in white wool.

Step 5: Wind thread to the head and follow with white wool. Tie off and trim.

Step 6: Rib the body with the tinsel. Tie off and trim.

Step 7: Cut a small bunch of fine olive-brown bucktail fibres and even tips with a hair stacker. It is best to tie this fly sparse so don't pick too large a bunch. Also, choose fine hairs as they will slick down into a more realistic silhouette than thick or coarse bucktails will.

Step 8: Tie in the bucktail just behind the hook with the tips facing forward. You want to be able to fold the hair back over the hook so that the tips extend about 1/4 inch beyond the end of the hook.

Step 9: Add a drop of glue and cover about 1/4 inch of the bucktail again with thread as you wind it back towards the eye. Trim off the butts where the body begins. Glue thread again.

Step 10: Tie in 4-6 pearlescent Crystal Hair strands over the bucktail.

Step 11: Cut a small bunch of fine, white bucktail, stack it and tie in on the bottom of the hook, reversing the vise to facilitate the process.

Step 12: Tie in 4-6 pearlescent Crystal Hair strands over the bucktail.

Step 13: Bring thread back to where the bucktail meets the body. Whip finish and cut. Tie in red thread.

Step 14: Stroke the bucktail fibers backwards so they lay over the top and bottom of the body, keeping the olive-brown and white fibers separate. With the red thread, tie down the bucktail fibres, making sure to keep them as tight as you can. Whip finish.

Step 15: Put the stick-on eyes on both sides of the head.

Step 16: Lightly coat the entire bucktail head with epoxy glue to keep the eyes on and add to durability.

Grizzly Seiler Fly

It's not every fly that gets developed in the kitchen sink, but that's the history behind the Grizzly Seiler, according to its inventor, Fred Seiler. "The large cutthroat just weren't taking our flies, so I tried to develop a fly which would imitate the chinook salmon fry's shape and colour," he said. "When I wet the fly in the sink, the black marabou looked just like the dark back of the fry and the shiny bear hair and tinsel suggested the flash of the fry's sides." As it is a larger fly, the Grizzly Seiler makes an excellent imitation of salmon smolts as well.

The Kitimat River was clear and cold as we began fishing one spring for sea-run cutthroat. I went through the pool first with a Grizzly Seiler on a floating line, and Seiler had on the intermediate sinking line he favours. I had worked my way down to the tailout without success, when I had a strong take as the fly swung into shore. The fish put up such a spirited fight, at first I thought it was a small steelhead, but when it rolled on the surface, I could see it was a good-sized cutthroat. When I landed the sea-run trout several minutes later, the Grizzly Seiler was firmly embedded in the corner of its mouth, testament to the fly's effectiveness in imitating the fry the trout was feeding on. After taking a few quick pictures, I released the fish into the dark pool, unharmed.

Because he values grizzly bears so much, he wanted me to stress that the hair he uses comes from an old grizzly bear rug he found. While Seiler likes the shine of bear hair, he said that any stiff hair such as deer or elk-hair tips would work. One of the main purposes in using the hair for the wing and tail is to keep the marabou from collapsing or wrapping around the hook, so it is important to use stiff hair.

Seiler ties two versions of the Grizzly Seiler, using the dark brown hair from the grizzly for one and the blonde hair for the other. In this way, he imitates the different salmon fry and smolts. Since he uses the fly for trout, Dollies and steelhead all year round, having dark and light variations makes it possible to respond to different

The Light Grizzly Seiler.

Photographed by Fred Seiler

Chapter Three: Fishing Salmon Alevin　　　　47

water and light conditions. Lately, he has been experimenting with a version that uses soft, black hackles for wings, resulting in a very slim, life-like silhouette. In its various forms, this simple, but effective, pattern is truly a fly for all seasons on coastal rivers, as you will find out if you give it a try.

Grizzly Seiler

HOOK: Tiemco salmon hook, #4
THREAD: Black 6/0
BODY: Silver Diamond Braid
TAIL: Blonde or dark brown grizzly bear hair or substitute
UNDERWING: Pearlescent Crystal Hair over blonde or dark brown grizzly bear hair or substitute
OVERWING: Black marabou or black hackles

TYING INSTRUCTIONS

Step 1: Tie in the hair from the head of the hook to the tail to create a smooth surface for the tinsel body. The tail should be as long as the shank of the hook.

Step 2: Take the thread back to the head, tie in the silver Diamond Braid, and wrap the tinsel to the tail and back to the head. Tie off and trim.

Step 3: Tie in a wing of matching hair almost as long as the tail. If desired, add half a dozen strands of pearlescent Crystal Hair over the hair wing.

Step 4: Tie in a thick wing of black marabou over the hair wing about the same length. Tie off and whip finish.

Fishing the Alevin and Fry Imitations

Water temperature is the key to the timing of salmon fry emergence. Sockeye juveniles emerge in April when valley bottom streams reach 10 degrees, but may not emerge until early June in higher-elevation waters, like the Babine's famous Rainbow Alley, where spring comes later. Experience and local knowledge will tell you which fry are around and when in your area.

It does not take long to learn to recognize the different salmon fry and to pick out fly patterns that match them. Slender, and silver sided with dark-green backs, pink fry head straight to the salt water, but because they are the most numerous of the salmon fry and tend to move in schools, it is worthwhile fishing an accurate imitation. Chum fry are similar to pinks but have parr marks and no dark-green back; they also head to the ocean on emergence and are available for a short period of time. Darker, with distinct parr marks and orange-edged tails and fins, coho fry reside in sloughs and backwaters for a year or more before migrating to the ocean, and a fry pattern can be fished all year round. Chinook are the largest of the fry and have variable residencies in fresh water. Their lower numbers mean that it is rarely necessary to use a close imitation.

The spring emergence of sockeye fry can create spectacular trout fishing on rivers where they spawn because of their abundance. Tommy Brayshaw developed the Yolk Sac with a light mallard wing, silver body and red throat hackle for the Adams River. Tying down the mallard at the bend and using red wool for the throat created the Egg 'n' I. The red hackle fibers or wool perhaps suggest the remnants of the egg sac or the red glow of the gills to the trout, but either way, it certainly enhances the fly. The mallard fiber wing is very fragile, so some fly tiers coat it lightly with epoxy for durability. Others tie a simple variation with painted or stick-on eyes and a tied-down wing of mallard dyed a dark green to imitate the pink fry.

The Rolled Muddler with its silver tinsel body, pale mallard flank wing and red throat of tying thread, makes a good all-round fry pattern for fishing in the surface film, especially when trout are slashing at the hapless fry drifting downstream.

Again, red for the throat seems to add to the fly's effectiveness. The standard pattern can be varied to good effect. When fish are feeding on injured fry tumbling along the bottom, a bead-head Muddler sinks down to where the trout are. When trout have keyed on coho fry, the tan version with woodduck flank wings and tail, and gold tinsel body is more effective. This darker version sometimes works better on bright days too as the original seems too flashy in the sunshine.

Too many times I see anglers who enjoyed the ease of the "duffer's week," when any silver fly fished quartering downstream worked, give up and go home when the trout refuse it later in the season. They are missing some of the best fishing of the year. These anglers need to try different fry patterns, different equipment, and a variety of fishing techniques until they find the ones that start hooking fish again.

In his book, *Fisherman's Spring*, Haig-Brown said that, despite his experimentation with different fry patterns, he was convinced that the type of movement and the depth at which the angler presents his fly are more important than the pattern itself, and recommends that the flyfisher try several different presentations, according to the season.

To facilitate the line control needed for different presentations, my preference in equipment is to fish as light a line as wind conditions and fly size will permit and to use a medium-long rod. I have three rods that I habitually use during the salmon hatch: an 8 1/2-foot split

Fishing for cutthroat in the spring.

cane #5 made by Bob Clay; a 9-foot Fenwick 4-weight graphite rod; and a 10-foot Sage 6-weight graphite rod. I like the longer, bigger rod while fishing rivers like the Stellako when it is windy on the river or when I need to cast large patterns, like the Stimulator, long distances, but the lighter weight rods are more fun to fish with, letting even a small trout show its stuff.

I fish with a full-floating line about 90% of the time, resorting to a clear "slime" line when water conditions are low and clear, and using a fast-sinking sink-tip only when the river is high and fast.

Holding Spots for Fry-Feeding Trout

During the peak of the fry hatch, trout can seem to be rising all over the river, but a little careful observation will reveal that in fact trout and char are holding in specific locations. These spots must not only provide ready access to the emerging salmon juveniles, they must also provide the trout and char with a sense of security, although when in a feeding frenzy, it sometimes seems that they have thrown security aside to take advantage of the fry feast.

When the pink and chum

salmon fry are migrating to salt water, they are poor swimmers and are carried downstream in the currents, wiggling futilely in the surface film. You will first notice this phenomenon when trout and Dollies start porpoising after the drifting fry, leaping repeatedly as they move downstream attacking a school of migrating juveniles. Schools of sockeye fry and smolts moving downstream can trigger this behavior too. Sometimes, you can see individual fish cruising the shallows, like small sharks, on the lookout for newly emerged and hapless fry. Other times you will notice—and often hear—large swirls as a large char or trout plucks a hapless fry off the surface of the water. These rises can be so explosive at times that they are really quite heart-stopping!

A holding spot has to offer fry-eating trout several important things: security from their predators, a location where fry are present in good numbers, and an opportunity to "ambush" their prey. Even in apparently open water, gravel bars, rocks and debris will create deeper seams and drop-offs where trout can lie in wait. If these are located below shallow, gravelly sections where the fry will emerge, all the better. Trout and char will hold on the downstream edge of gravel bars, along the edges of rocks and sunken logs, and under the riffly water of tailouts, waiting for the little salmon to be swept downstream in the currents. In one of my favorite rivers, I can tell when the hatch is on because I will see splashes in these locations, but the bigger fish are sometimes more discrete than their smaller cousins, making little or no commotion when they take a fry.

On a typical day one spring, I arrived at my favorite home stream and immediately noticed splashy rises in the open flats, a dead giveaway that trout were feeding on fry. This was confirmed when I saw several trout splash once, then porpoise on the surface slightly downstream from the first rise and then splash noisily further downstream yet again. As I waded out above the flats where I had seen the first rises, I saw much smaller, more discreet rises in the swirling currents below gravel bars and at the end of short, rocky rapid sections of the stream. Finally, I could see the occasional almost imperceptible swirl beside log jams along the stream bank. To an observant angler it was obvious that trout and char were feeding actively on fry throughout the river.

Knowing where trout will be located while they are feeding is the first important key to successful-fishing the salmon hatch. The next are fishing the right salmon-fry imitation and doing it in the way the trout expect to see the fry. I decided to first target a small rise I had seen in the turbulence where the stream flowed over a shallow gravel bar. The water was three to four feet deep on the downstream side, but less than a foot above the bar. A trout would have an excellent opportunity to spy a drifting fry in the shallow water and to attack it before it escaped into deeper water. The foamy currents on the surface and the deep water behind the bar provided a perfect haven for trout.

Chapter Three: Fishing Salmon Alevin

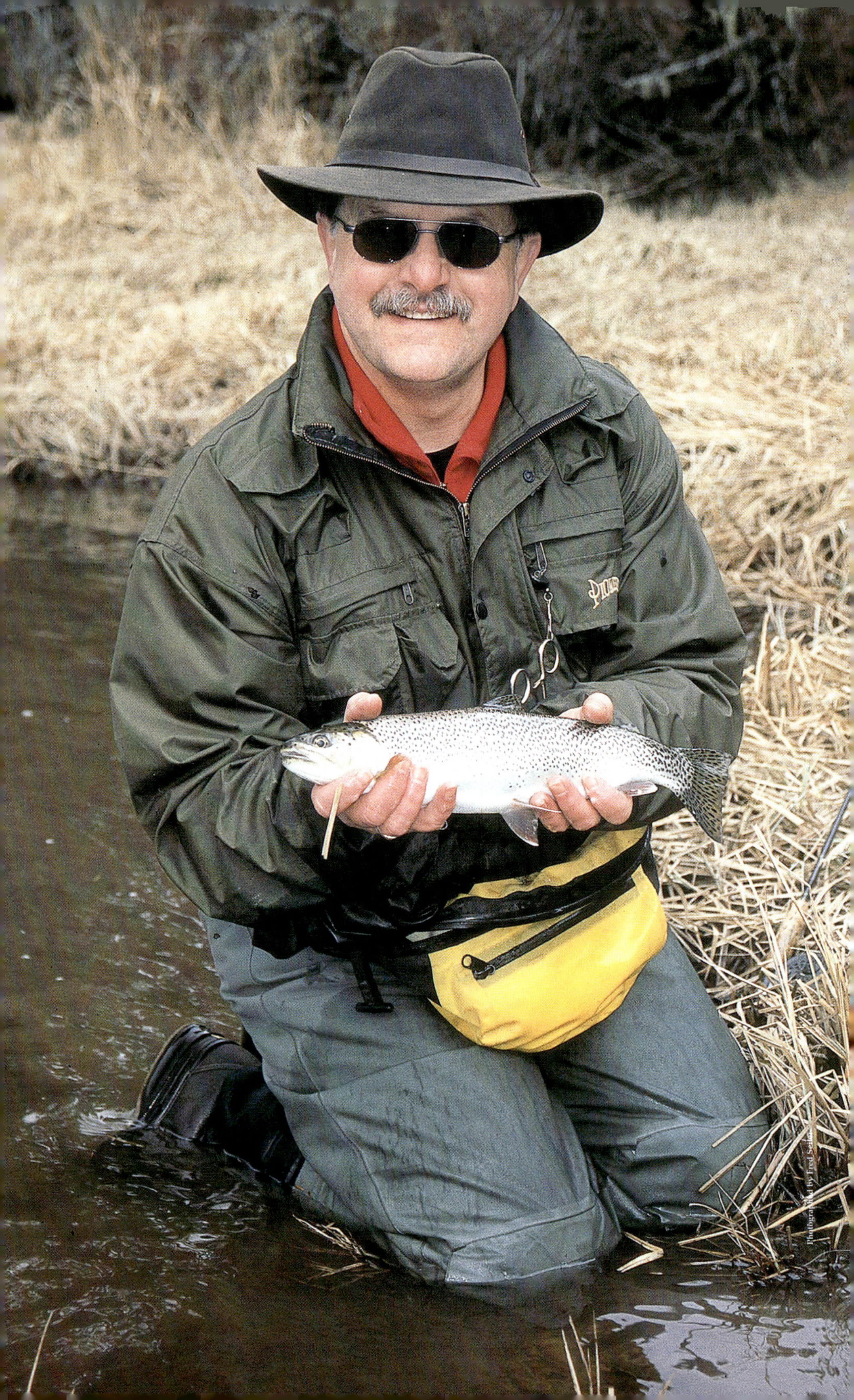

A Dolly Varden char caught in the spring on an epoxy fry pattern.

I tied on a silvery pink salmon-fry imitation and cast above the shoal, letting the fly swing across the bar into the swirling currents below. As the fly began to drag slightly across the currents, it was met with a sudden strong take, and I realized that I had completely underestimated the size of the trout I had seen rise. It was obvious from the start that this was a rainbow trout for it fought much harder than a cutthroat and seemed to spend as much time in the air as in the water at first. For several minutes I had my hands full trying to bring the fish to the net, and when I did, it turned out to be a 20-plus-inch fish weighing over four pounds, my largest rainbow from that river.

I carried on wading downstream and took more fish where they were holding along the edge of a deeper, faster seam of water; within inches of a sunken log where a big cutthroat trout was hiding in the dark, quiet current; from beneath an overhanging tree where a deeper pool provided additional protection; and in a fast riffle beside a large rock where another large rainbow trout snatched a drifting fry from the surface. Knowing where the fish are located is critical to being able to put your imitation in front of them. Using the right technique so that it is presented naturally to the trout is the next goal.

Facing Page: Author with a spring cuttie

Chapter Three: Fishing Salmon Alevin

Here are some methods I have experimented with and which have all been productive at different times.

Floating Line Techniques

While it is relatively easy to teach a beginner to fly cast, teaching him or her how to actually fish, that is to control the fly well enough to catch fish, is sometimes much more difficult. The early weeks of the salmon fry hatch are one of the few times when rivers are so full of willing trout that even a rank beginner can gain confidence in his ability to catch fish on the fly. When the fish are this eager, you rarely need anything more than a floating line and a small silvery streamer like a Rolled Muddler. Line control is relatively easy most of the time too, with the traditional downstream wet-fly swing working well enough at least to keep the beginner busy catching trout.

Haig-Brown clearly tried each time he was fishing fry patterns to find the retrieve that worked best that day. He said use a fast strip on the surface when trout were slashing at fleeing fry; a deep, rolling retrieve in the early spring when alevin were emerging; a slow, smooth, deep retrieve later when there were still few fry about; and a greased-line approach with a slim fly and little movement in the late summer for what he called "big harvest cutthroats." He mentions varying the speed and rhythm of the retrieve as well as the depth by stripping in the fly, varying the angle of the cast upstream or downstream, and by moving the rod tip, but he admits that he has experienced those frustrating times that all anglers know when trout are rising to fry all around him, but refusing his presentations. There are no guarantees in fly-fishing, and that is part of its appeal, but every angler should be familiar with the different ways of presenting the fry patterns to the trout, because the more you experiment, the more likely you are to find the one that works on a given day.

The Traditional Wet-Fly Swing

The old "chuck-and-chance-it" wet-fly technique is still a popular and effective method of fishing during much of the salmon-fry hatch. It is a good way of exploring unfamiliar water and covering as much water as possible. Cast quartering (45 degrees) downstream towards either bank and mend upstream slightly to ensure that you stay in touch with the fly as it swings below you. The traditional wet-fly presentation works well in spots where you can cast above fish holding on the edge of the current and let your fly swing across the current and past the fish.

It is harder in some ways to control a wet fly than a dry fly because you cannot see what it's doing below the surface of the water. If you try to cast across several currents, the fly will be dragged by the currents, come to the surface, and race past the fish too fast to look natural. So try to locate yourself where you can avoid this. Avoid the temptation to cast too far as well: it is much harder to stay in touch with the wet fly if you have a lot of line out and to set the hook if you have a lot of slack. It has been my experience that trout feeding on fry are far less likely to be frightened by a wading angler. Indeed, on numerous occasions I have had trout splash noisily within a rod's length away from me when they were intent on the fry.

Dead Drift

Most of the time trout expect to see newly hatched fry drifting downstream in the current. Oblige them by fishing your lightly sinking imitation (not floating) like a dry fly: cast quartering upstream, mend the line upstream, and continue to strip in enough line to stay in touch with the fry, as you would a freely drifting dry fly. Keep your rod high and as much line out of the water, so that the different currents do not drag your fly unnaturally. You want your fly to float in the surface film, not on it, so a Rolled Muddler, if tied properly, or another light streamer pattern, is ideal for this type of fishing. There should be a small, spare deer-hair head and only a few strands of deer hair in the wing so that the Muddler does not skate across the surface, but rather drifts in it like a hapless natural.

You can extend the dead drift down below you by releasing more line from your left hand. Fishing this way presents the fly sideways to the trout and is very similar to the "greased line" presentation that Atlantic salmon and steelhead anglers have adopted from Arthur Wood, and to which Haig-Brown refers.

Cuttie.

Chapter Three: Fishing Salmon Alevin

This technique works well for trout holding in drop-offs, deep runs and below gravel bars where they can ambush the fry popping out of the gravel beds. Cast up above in the shallow water and let the fly drift naturally over the drop-off or into the deeper seam. Strike fast and hard, because with the dead-drift retrieve, trout rarely hook themselves.

"Speed Up"

There are times when this variation on the dead drift works wonders on reluctant trout. Cast upstream above a fish that has shown itself, but, instead of mending upstream as with the dead drift, mend the line downstream to let the line bow, and the current accelerate the fly downstream. The fry pattern will dart towards the trout and swing enticingly away, triggering a chase reflex. I've found this to be an especially effective retrieve in the darkening hours of the evening: the large trout, and especially Dolly Varden, move into the shallows along the stream's borders waiting to ambush emerging fry. With the speed-up retrieve, the fry imitation approaches the trout downstream as they expect, and its faster movement as it swings past them spurs the predatory chase response. Vary the speed by stripping in line. You won't have to worry about setting the hook: trout and char that miss the escaping fly will frequently chase it and swipe at it several times before hooking themselves.

I've caught some of my biggest cutthroat trout using this technique in holding spots that would be impossible to fish with any other method: the quiet water behind sunken logs or large boulders. Casting a Rolled Muddler into the patch of still water between the current and the obstruction, and then letting the current pull it across the spot has resulted in some exciting takes as a large trout has chased the fleeing "fry" and taken it before it escaped into the fast flow.

Skittering

Just before dark, large cutthroat and Dolly Varden that ignored your flies all day abandon all caution, slashing wildly at anything that moves. Cast a floating fly like the Rolled Muddler quartering downstream on a short line and let the fly skitter across the surface in front of where you saw a feeding trout by holding your rod tip up. This is just like skating a surface fly for steelhead: you want the fly to wake in the surface slowly enough that the fish will be able to catch it and hook itself, but fast enough to stimulate the chase instinct. A warning: cut back to a 3X or even 2X tippet; the fish can be big at this time of day! One evening on a Skeena tributary, I landed a 20-inch cutthroat and a 24-inch Dolly by skittering my fly through the riffles. When that big Dolly hit and took off downstream, I was sure I had on a late-spring steelhead.

This technique works well over fish that have seen lots of flies too. I think that one way the trout come to distinguish between an imitation and a real fry is by the little wake the natural makes as it struggles in the surface film. Or maybe the wake just makes it easier for the trout to target its quarry. Either way, it is quite

A beautifully colored cuttie on a sockeye fry.

exciting to witness the aggressive take of a large fish to a waking fry pattern: it is almost as much fun as fishing the dry fly.

An important, if somewhat tricky, variation of skittering the fry pattern is to cast it slightly upstream of the feeding trout and by holding the rod high, skate it downstream and across the current in front of the fish. This is about the only way I know of effectively imitating a struggling salmon fry being swept downstream in the current. Be ready for an explosive take with this approach because the trout and char come rocketing off the bottom after the fly.

Hang Down

When cutthroat and rainbow trout are holding on the edge of fast water, waiting for a fry to struggle out of the current into the quiet eddy, they will often take a fry pattern swinging in the current below the angler. The regular wet-fly swing imitates this movement, but a more natural presentation can be achieved by feeding line so that the fly drifts, tail downstream like the real thing, into the feeding fish. Although it sometimes seems like trout are moving all around when you see so many rises to the fry, often the individual fish are holding in one place and letting their dinner drift down to them. Mark these locations and get above these feeding fish to use the hang-down method.

Cast downstream towards the trout, stopping your line suddenly in the air to create a slack line. Then let the fly drift with the current towards the waiting trout, feeding line if necessary. This technique imitates the

Chapter Three: Fishing Salmon Alevin

frantic movement of the natural fry as it drifts downstream, with its tail wiggling futilely. The Chickabou Fry is especially suited to this method of fishing because the marabou tail flutters in the current like the real thing.

This is a popular technique on rivers like the Babine where it is permissible to fish from boats. Anchor the boat above feeding fish and cast out enough line to reach the fish. Let the line rest on the surface and the fly swing backwards and forwards below you. You can further entice the fish by raising the rod tip, lowering it and letting the fly drift back down naturally to the trout. Twitching the fly also enhances this presentation and helps trigger violent takes. One problem with this approach is that with the fish taking the fly directly downstream of you, if you strike quickly upwards as you would normally do, you are likely to lift the fly right out of the fish's mouth or at least set the hook in the

The salmon feed the eagles too.

front of the mouth, one of the most likely spots to pull out. It is also easy to pop off a big fish this way. A solution is to set the hook by striking sideways instead of by lifting the rod straight up.

Targeting

When schools of fry are drifting downstream, trout slash at them, porpoising repeatedly as they follow the school. They are trying to injure one of the passing fry and will swirl back to pick off the victims. When this is happening, I keep a floating line in the air, false casting, and quickly-emphasis on quickly-cast my fly just downstream of the last boil on the surface. As soon as the fly hits the water and sinks, I give it several sharp tugs and that is all that is required most times to convince a hungry cutthroat or rainbow that my fly is the little salmon it had injured in its attack.

"Nymphing" With Weighted Flies

When there is little or no surface activity, especially if there is bright light on the water, fish down on the gravel to get results. Cast a weighted Storey's Alevin, Chickabou Fry or Grizzly Seiler upstream, mend upstream and let it sink, as you would a weighted stonefly nymph. Hold the rod high, retrieving slack to stay in touch with the sunk fly and as the fly drifts by you, ticking bottom, feed out line to extend the natural drift. I suspect this technique imitates the many dead and injured alevin and fry rolling along the bottom in the current, and it often makes the difference in hooking the larger, wilier trout. As Haig-Brown observed, this is a good approach to try early in the spring when the water is cold, trout are sluggish and the alevin are tumbling along the stream bottom.

Boat Techniques

As I mentioned, several techniques like the "hang down" can be adapted to fishing from anchored boats, but there are other effective ways of fishing the fry imitation that can only be used from freely drifting boats.

The "Dead Drift" Boat

While it is possible to dead drift the salmon-fry pattern from an anchored boat, it is often difficult to get a long drift because of the multiple currents pulling on your line. A popular way to overcome this is a method adapted from drift-boat fishers who use grasshopper patterns. Let the boat drift freely downstream perhaps with someone guiding it with a paddle, while the fly-fishers cast out and let their fly drift naturally downstream in synchronization with the boat.

Depending on the wind and currents, your boat may drift more slowly or faster than the line, so you may need to recast and keep taking in slack to stay connected to your fly. Rises to the free-floating fry pattern can be surprisingly explosive as a trout streaks to the surface to intercept the imitation.

"Trolling"

This is the ultimate lazy man's way of fishing, I admit. On a recent trip, I caught several good fish drifting downstream in my inflatable kayak with the fly dragging behind me on a

A spring cutthroat on a pink salmon fry.

taut line. The little wake the Rolled Muddler made on the surface as it was pulled across the currents imitated a fleeing fry and brought a slashing strike from the pursuing trout.

Spot Casting

This really is like grasshopper fishing. When trout are actively feeding, as the boat drifts downstream, keep the floating line and fly in the air, and be ready when a trout rises within casting distance, to cast quickly into the circle of the rise. A trout feeding on a moving school of fish will follow them downstream, slashing repeatedly again and again at the surface. This gives you several chances to target the fish. A quick tug of your line when the fly has landed will create the wake of a fleeing fry and stimulate a strike.

Sinking-Line Techniques

Using the floating-line techniques is in many ways the most satisfying method of fishing fry patterns because it is exciting to see the fish take on the surface, but there are many occasions when there is no obvious surface activity and the floating line is not effective. During the middle of the day or in the early spring when there are fewer fry around, it is worthwhile switching to a sinking line and getting your fly down deep to where the trout are still feeding on the emerging alevin or injured fry that roll along the river bottom. When the traditional wet-fly swing with a sinking line does not produce cutthroat or rainbow trout for you during the fry hatch, be prepared to experiment with different flies and sinking-line techniques and you will be pleasantly surprised by the results.

The Traditional Wet-Fly Swing

Heavy runoff in early spring or several days of rain can quickly turn a coastal river into a turbid, raging torrent. When the river is deep and the current strong, a fast-sinking line with a weighted fly on a short leader provides the enticing movement and depth that can make the difference between getting skunked and having a memorable day. Remember to slow down the drift of the fly in the cold, fast waters to get your fly right down onto the gravel bottom, and give the trout as much time as possible to see and react to your fry imitation. Hapless newly emerged alevin, and injured or dead fry will roll and tumble slowly in the slower current just above the streambed, and trout and char will feast on this easy meal.

When the water is really high and fast, it is necessary to cast upstream with a fast-sinking line or shooting head and mend upstream several times to let the line get right down to the stream bed. Fish slow and deep. The longer you are able to keep the fry pattern in the view of a trout in the cold, fast water of early spring, the better your chances of getting it to bite.

The "Hang Down" Technique

The basic principle of this sinking-line approach is a variation of the same method with a floating line. This is a popular and effective technique in rivers where fishing from anchored boats is legal. Anchor or wade into a position above feeding trout. Using a fast-sinking shooting head or full-sinking line, false cast enough line to get down to the fish, and then stop your cast short, allowing the line to collapse into the water. The line will sink quickly in the current and drift down towards the feeding fish. If you have judged the distance correctly, the fly will swing enticingly backwards and forwards in the current in front of the fish.

In a strong current, this technique is almost like trolling, since the current keeps the fly in constant motion. Its only disadvantage is that trout often nip at the fly and can be more difficult to hook if they take the fly directly downstream from you because your strike will be pulling it out of their mouths. Make sure your hooks are super sharp, and if you miss several strikes, twitch or pull the fly, this will sometimes entice a reluctant fish to smash the fly.

Stripping In

Large fish, especially Dolly Varden char and bull trout, are piscivorous, feeding almost exclusively on sticklebacks, minnows and salmon fry. A fleeing baitfish triggers the hunter's instinct in them and they will give chase to it, snatching at it several times until they finally connect. When a deeply sunk, dead-drifted fry pattern has failed to draw a strike, try stripping the fly in. Vary the speed of the retrieve, letting the fly stop and sway in the currents before stripping it in again. Be prepared for some violent strikes.

CHAPTER FOUR

Salmon Caviar

The Moveable Feast

Above the still waters of Shuswap Lake the first dusting of snow covered the ponderosa pine trees and sagebrush bushes. It was mid October and I was fishing the mouth of the Adams River, home of one of British Columbia's most famous sockeye salmon runs. I and several other anglers were standing on the wide delta of the Adams where it fans out into Shuswap Lake. The braided channels were shallow enough for us to wade across, and as we did, we passed thousands upon thousands of bright red and green sockeye intent on laying their eggs in the gravel. We weren't interested in the salmon, however. What we were fishing for were the large, silvery rainbow trout that were feasting on a banquet of red-orange sockeye eggs.

Thousands of visitors are drawn to Roderick Haig-Brown Provincial Park to witness the spectacle of the returning Adams River sockeye, especially during the dominant four-year run, when upwards of 2 million fish make it to the spawning beds, in addition to the 8 million that are intercepted by the commercial salmon fleet. These plucky fish first entered fresh water in the estuary of the Fraser River at Vancouver, battled its powerful currents upstream to Lytton, turned east to follow the Thompson past Kamloops, and then travelled onto Shuswap Lake and the Adams

River, a journey of over 300 miles.

The run was almost wiped out in 1913 when a slide at Hell's Gate, triggered by railway construction, blocked the Fraser. The Salmon River, another tributary of Shuswap Lake, lost its run, but enough Adams River fish got through to save the run. Studies have shown that eggs are a significant part of the diet of rainbow trout in Shuswap Lake, for example, and that rainbow trout will follow migrating salmon all the way from the Thompson River and grow fat on the eggs that are swept downstream and into the lake. They stay in the lake to feed in the fall on the flesh of the dead adults and in the spring on the fry and smolts as they leave the Adams to enter the lake.

I was going to take advantage of that fact by fishing a bright red-orange egg fly and I had several patterns to choose from: a simple Jensen egg tied on with a little white marabou; a weighted chenille pattern; and the venerable Glo Bug. The river water in the delta was so low that the backs of the spawning sockeye were exposed to the air and so clear it was easy to see if any trout were around. I didn't see any in the river itself, so I began concentrating on the edge of the gravel where it dropped off into the lake. I noticed several bright, silvery flashes in the darker water, and could hardly believe my eyes when a large rainbow trout zipped out of the lake and aggressively bumped into the side of one of the salmon. Then the trout drifted back into the lake. This scene was repeated several times, and then I realized what the trout was doing: it was dislodging eggs by bumping the belly of the female sockeye and then following the eggs downstream, eating them along the way.

I tied on a Glo Bug, added a small split shot about 18 inches up the leader, cast the fly just above the salmon, and mended upstream. It drifted past her as she turned on her side and dug out a redd with her tail, drifted to the edge of the drop-off, and disappeared into the lake. I fed out the floating fly line and it followed the river currents out about twenty feet, and then the fly line dipped suddenly. I set the hook and felt the pull of a good fish. Moments later, a bright rainbow trout about 18 inches long threw itself into the air, dove and streaked off, heading for safety of deeper water. I brought it to the net and marvelled at its slim, silvery, superb condition. It looked like a small steelhead—and it had fought like one, jumping repeatedly.

That day I caught a dozen or more trout in similar fashion and they were all 18 inches or better, good fish under any circumstances. I tried a variety of egg flies and they all worked, but the key was presenting them dead drift, just like the natural eggs that tumbled downstream in the currents.

The small gravel of the Adams River provides the ideal spawning conditions for sockeye. The female turns on her side and digs a depression in the gravel by rapidly flexing her body and tail so that sand, debris and fine gravel are swept downstream in the current. She lays her eggs—from 500 to a 1000 in each nest—and after the male has fertilized them, covers them through further digging. This process will be repeated four or five times at the redd site. The female will stay near the redd to protect her eggs until she dies. The eggs

Coho salmon eggs scattered by a feeding bear.

are temporarily sticky after being deposited and this helps them adhere to the gravel. There shell hardens quickly on contact with the water, but they remain vulnerable to crushing until the "eyed" stage. The eggs that escape from the nest to drift downstream soon lose their deep colouring and translucent appearance, turning a milky-pink colour.

British Columbia has quite a few lake systems that support sockeye and provide river mouth fishing for big trout and Dolly Varden char feeding on the salmon eggs. In the north of the province, Meziadin, Lakelse, and Babine lakes provide good fishing where spawning creeks enter the lakes or where rivers drain them. Further east, where the Stellako River connects Francois and Fraser lakes is an important spawning area and Quesnel, Chilko and Shuswap lake trout also enter nearby rivers with the coming of spawning sockeye in September. In Alaska, the Bristol Bay area is home to several dozen sockeye lake systems, including Iliamna Lake, the largest sockeye-producing lake in the world. On the whole, the Bristol Bay lakes are relatively close to tidal water and at a low elevation, so the sockeye arrive quickly, over a two-week period. Rainbow trout up to ten pounds feed on the salmon eggs in these rivers. Of the eight lake systems that used to produce more than a million sockeye on the Columbia River in Washington State, only three are productive today: Wenatchee, Quinault and Washington.

Most of these rivers also support chinook, coho and pink salmon and the trout will be feeding on the free-floating eggs from these other species too. Sockeye eggs are easy to identify, however, and when the trout are keying in on them it is important to match them in size and color. Sockeye eggs can be distinguished from other salmon eggs by their smaller size and dark red-orange color. The eggs are about 6 mm in diameter and relatively transparent. Pink and chum eggs are a lighter orange, with chum and chinook eggs being much larger. Coho eggs are more opaque. Not only does the sockeye female produce the smallest eggs, she also produces the highest number for body weight, ranging from 2,000 to 5,000. By contrast, pinks carry around 1,500; chinook less than 2,000; and coho about 2,500.

Full of proteins, carbohydrates, minerals and vitamins, the yolks of sockeye and other salmon eggs provide the basis of life for the developing salmon juveniles and are a nutritious feast for the trout, char, whitefish, sculpins and other creatures that feed on them. The trout not only hang around spawning females, trying to dart in and snatch freshly extruded eggs, they also hold below the schools of salmon, waiting for loose, drifting eggs. Although the quick burial of the nest after laying the eggs reduces the number that are not safely deposited in the gravel, some do get carried downstream in the currents. Also, late-spawning fish can dig up existing redds and scatter already deposited eggs. Rainbow and cutthroat trout and Dolly Varden char will locate themselves near the salmon redds to take advantage of this phenomenon.

The sheer quantity of salmon eggs in healthy rivers was made clear to me one fall on the Kispiox River when several weeks of heavy rains turned the waters churning brown. The river overflowed its banks forcing thousands of pink salmon to spawn in the flooded rodeo grounds. When the waters receded, the ground looked like it had been covered in pale pink hailstones, millions of pink salmon eggs that would never have the chance to develop. It was obvious that the eggs of the pink and other salmon species were incredibly numerous and represented a major food source for the predatory fish in the river.

Early attempts to imitate salmon caviar relied on chenille bodies, but recently, yarn, various plastics and hot glue guns have been used to create more and more realistic egg patterns.

Traditional Egg Patterns

Babine Special

One could easily argue that many of the early steelhead flies with their fluorescent orange and red chenille bodies, like the Polar Shrimp and Kispiox Special, are in fact egg patterns, but one of the first flies to be tied as a clear imitation of salmon eggs was the Babine Special. Developed for late-fall steelhead on the Babine River in British Columbia, it is still an effective egg fly and will take trout where salmon are spawning.

HOOK:	Atlantic salmon hook, #4-6
THREAD:	Black 6/0
TAIL:	A clump of white marabou fibers
REAR EGGS:	Large fluorescent orange chenille built up into a ball shape
MIDDLE HACKLE:	Red hackle
FRONT EGG:	Large fluorescent red chenille built up into a ball shape
COLLAR HACKLE:	White hackle, slightly larger than the middle hackle

Double-Egg Sperm Fly

Dave Whitlock developed this egg pattern in the '60s for steelhead fishing in Alaska. The egg size is more realistic than in the Babine Special, but the fly is tied more like a traditional Atlantic salmon pattern with a tag and golden pheasant crest tail.

HOOK:	Atlantic salmon hook, #4-6
THREAD:	Fluorescent orange 6/0
TAG:	Medium, flat gold tinsel
TAIL:	Golden pheasant crest
BODY:	Two balls of fluorescent orange chenille separated by flat gold tinsel
COLLAR HACKLE:	Fluorescent orange hackle
WING:	White marabou tied over the hackle

Newer Egg Patterns

Float fishermen often catch steelhead and salmon on a simple egg imitation that consists of a few strands of fluorescent egg yarn tied to a hook. Fly-fishermen began experimenting with this material and one pattern emerged which is almost guaranteed to catch trout, even when there are no eggs around—the Glo Bug.

Glo Bug

HOOK: A variety of hooks are used for this pattern. One of the most popular is the gold-plated egg hook in #4-8 used by bait-fishermen, but any heavy, wide-gaped, short-shanked hook will work. A popular choice is the Dai Riki #135.

THREAD: Heavy duty, at least 3/0 in colours to match the body

BODY: Four pieces of orange, pink, red or yellow egg yarn tied down onto the hook shank to flare them out, trimmed with scissors into an egg shape. A popular variation is to make one of the strands fluorescent red to suggest the darker, oil spot in fresh eggs.

Pom-Pom "Fly"

I frequently raid the local craft shop for fly-tying materials and one of the ones I came across was bags of acrylic yarn decorative pom-poms in various sizes and colours. These little balls are basically several strands of yarn held together with a staple. They can be bought in white if you want to dye your own eggs, or in pink, orange and red to match the various salmon eggs. They can also be purchased with Mylar sparkle incorporated into the body to add a little more flash.

The pom-poms can be attached to a hook by simply sliding the point through the centre of the staple, or by threading a piece of monofilament or heavy thread through the staple with a needle. Either way, they make a great salmon egg and can be tied on the hook individually or in a clump. You could not ask for an easier fly to create.

Chapter Four: Salmon Caviar: The Moveable Feast

CHAPTER FIVE

Fishing Egg Patterns

Trout and char grow big on the smorgasbord of salmon eggs that floats down Pacific Northwest rivers in the late summer and fall, as I discovered one day on the Kispiox. Wading downstream, I disturbed the loose pink salmon eggs that blanketed the stream bottom. I was

Cannibal Trout

watching the current lift them up and carry them away below me when I noticed the flash of a large fish in a deep bend close to shore. I realized it was probably the biggest Dolly Varden I had ever seen in the river, so I walked down the shoreline to a position above it where I could cast my egg fly to drift into the fish. I watched him inhale one drifting egg after another and repeatedly ignore my pale pink artificial. It took awhile to convince him to accept my counterfeit egg, but finally he grabbed it. When I brought him to shore, he was 27 inches long, as thick as my forearm and weighed about six pounds.

Even steelhead are not immune to salmon caviar. Roe bags are one of the deadliest baits for steelhead and they are also frequently taken on egg flies, like the Babine Special, which were developed specifically to imitate salmon eggs. Several times I have been fishing with egg patterns for trout behind spawning coho in the fall and been surprised by the violent take of a powerful, chrome-bright steelhead that quickly made a mockery of my attempts to control it on my 5-weight trout rod.

The Skeena River: home to all five species of Pacific salmon.

Chapter Five: Fishing Egg Patterns

CHAPTER SIX

Salmon Flesh
Tying and Fishing its Imitation

Illustration by Andrew Williams

Even after death salmon provide an important source of food for trout and char, as well as other living creatures. One late-fall day, I began fishing for trout below the colored and ragged coho that were spawning on the gravelly flats. The shoreline and shallows were littered with the rotting carcases of thousands of pink salmon whose spawning had preceded the cohos'. As they dug their redds, the coho stirred up these corpses and released strands of white flesh that floated downstream to the delight of several hundred mergansers. I carried on downstream intent on finding feeding trout, until I came to a deep pool formed at the confluence of a tributary. In fact, I was so intent on my search that I did not notice at first that I had company: a huge chocolate brown grizzly was sharing the pool with me. He would sink his head repeatedly into the pool, grab a fungus-covered dead pink and suck it up like a salmon milkshake. I was only too happy to retreat politely and leave him to his revolting repast.

I had taken several trout on egg patterns, having guessed that coho eggs were drifting down from the spawning beds upstream, but without consistent success. So, I switched to a simple salmon-flesh pattern, a beige and pink Bunny Leech. The decision paid off because as I waded to the tailout of the long pool, I caught one cutthroat trout and Dolly Varden after another that clearly shared the big bruin's taste for salmon flesh.

Alaskan fly-fishermen have known for a long time that rotting salmon flesh is one of the most important sources of protein for rainbow trout and Dolly Varden, providing them with one last, nourishing feast before the onset of winter. To imitate this vital food source, guides have developed a variety of flesh patterns that have proven effective in taking the huge resident Alaskan rainbows.

In heavily fished areas, fishermen also unwittingly add to the trout's' diet by cleaning their salmon along the streamside. On the Babine, for example, I have witnessed anglers cleaning their sockeye and the discarded eggs and bits of fresh flesh that floated downstream created a trout feeding frenzy to rival that of piranhas. When this is happening, flesh flies in brighter oranges and pinks are the ticket. At other times, especially later in the season, when the naturally rotting carcases release their flesh, white and the paler hues of beige, pink and orange more effectively imitate the drifting pieces of salmon on which the trout are feeding.

A rotting chum salmon releases flesh into the river.

Chapter Six: Salmon Flesh

Tying Simple Salmon-Flesh Flies

Most flesh flies are easy to tie and make use of readily available materials such as marabou, rabbit fur or yarn. Zonkers, Woolly Buggers, Bunny Leeches and Alaskabou streamers tied in the appropriate colors all make effective imitations of decaying salmon flesh drifting in the current. An angler fishing Pacific Northwest rivers in the later summer and fall should have a selection of patterns, sizes and colors available for the times when trout and char are gorging on the remains of spawned-out salmon.

Zonker

This streamer pattern designed to be a baitfish imitation is very suggestive of a piece of salmon flesh when tied in off-white, beige, or pale ginger, pink or orange. The silhouette and movement of the rabbit-fur body and tail match an undulating strip of flesh in the currents.

HOOK: Mustad 79850, #8 or #6
THREAD: 6/0 thread matching body color
BODY: Chenille or yarn in off-white, beige, ginger, or pale pink or orange. Add wraps of lead wire to weight the fly before completing the body
WING/TAIL: Strip of rabbit fur matching body color tied in at the bend of the hook to make the tail, laid over the top of the body and tied off at the head
HACKLE: Webby soft hackle tied in the round in matching color

Woolly Bugger

If there ever was a universal fly, the Woolly Bugger is probably the closest thing to it. In darker colors, it imitates everything from large nymphs to leeches and baitfish, and in paler colors it makes an excellent flesh fly. Adding a few wraps of fluorescent pink or orange chenille to the head creates the Egg Sucking Leech, so it is possible to imitate the two major sources of trout food during the salmon spawning season-eggs and salmon flesh.

HOOK: Mustad 79850, #8 or #6
THREAD: 6/0 thread matching body color
TAIL: Marabou and a few strands of Crystal Hair

Cannibal Trout

BODY: matching the body color Chenille or yarn in off-white, beige, ginger, or pale pink or orange. Add wraps of lead wire to weight the fly before completing the body
RIBBING: Medium silver oval tinsel
HACKLE: Schlappen hackle tied along the body in matching color

Bunny Leech

The flowing movements of rabbit fur in the water are enticing to fish and the Bunny Leech has become popular with trout anglers as a result. There are several variations of this simple and durable fly that are suggestive of a chunk of salmon flesh. The simplest involves making the tail and body of a single strip of cross-cut rabbit fur, with part of the strip left dangling for the tail and the rest wrapped around the hook and tied off at the head. A common variation is to make a tail of darker marabou or rabbit fur, in beige or orange, and carry on with a paler rabbit strip for the body. A few strands of Crystal Hair in a matching color add a little sparkle.

HOOK: Mustad 79850, #8 or #6 or similar hook
THREAD: 6/0 thread matching body color
TAIL: A section of rabbit fur or marabou as long as the body, either in the same color or in beige or pale orange
BODY: A strip of cross-cut rabbit fur in off-white, beige, ginger, or pale pink or orange wrapped around the shank of the hook and tied off at the head. Add wraps of lead wire to weight the fly before completing the body

Marabou Streamers

The Alaskabou streamer series of flies was developed in Alaska for salmon and steelhead, and the pulsating action of the marabou in versions like the Popsicle have proven themselves effective in rivers throughout the Northwest. By replacing the bright purples, reds and oranges of the original series with more muted shades or cream, pink, pale orange or brown, anglers can create a multi-hued flesh fly that looks very natural.

Chapter Six: Salmon Flesh

HOOK: 1/0-#6 Atlantic salmon hook
THREAD: 6/0 fluorescent orange
BODY: None
WING: Dark brown marabou tied in about 1/3 of the way back from the head, followed by two wraps each of pale orange, pale pink and white marabou.

Fishing Flesh Flies

The currents will tumble along the stream bed the bits and pieces of salmon flesh that have broken loose from the rotting bodies of the dead salmon, so this is where trout expect to intercept these scraps. Divers have witnessed schools of large rainbow trout tearing like a pack of wolves at salmon carcasses snagged by dead heads and sunken branches, but since it is impossible to imitate this situation, the angler's main concern should be in presenting his flesh fly in a manner that imitates the drift of the loose bits of flesh. The best way to do this is to fish these patterns on a dead drift, either with a floating line and weighted fly, or on a fast-sinking line.

In shallower water, such as tailouts of pools or the gravel spawning beds, a floating line is all that is necessary to present the flesh fly on a dead drift. Using a weighted fly with a strike indicator on the leader makes it easier to stay in touch with the fly as it drifts downstream and to see the take. Casting is more like a slow lob with this setup, but cast upstream, mend the line upstream to let the fly sink, and follow the strike indicator as it comes towards you. If the fly repeatedly snags bottom, shorten the distance between the indicator and the fly: you want it to tumble along the bottom, not get caught up in the rocks.

Trout feeding on salmon flesh will also frequently hold at the end of riffles or the heads of pools where loose bits of flesh will drop out of the currents into quieter water. These places are easy to identify because there are lots of salmon carcasses lying on the river bottom or along the edges. Water like this is best fished with a sinking line and a short leader. Stand upstream in the rapids, cast across the currents and let the fly swing into the edge of the current where the trout are holding.

One early fall on the Lakelse River, we discovered just such a spot. We were fishing below spawning gravel, looking for fall cutthroat trout and Dolly Varden, but our egg patterns had gone untouched. In a bend in the river where a long, shallow rapids dropped off into a deeper pool, we saw trout splashing along the edge of the current. My fishing partner, Clayton, put on a pale yellow marabou streamer and drifted it into the pool. Over the next hour, he caught a half a dozen chunky trout and char that had obviously been gorging on the smorgasbord of salmon flesh that had been drifting down from the carcasses that carpeted the river bottom.

Anglers in British Columbia, unlike their Alaskan counterparts, have been slow to take to fishing with flesh flies, but they should give these simple patterns a try in the postspawning season because they will discover that trout love them.

Facing page: Maggots break down a rotting salmon corpse.
photo by Fred Seiler

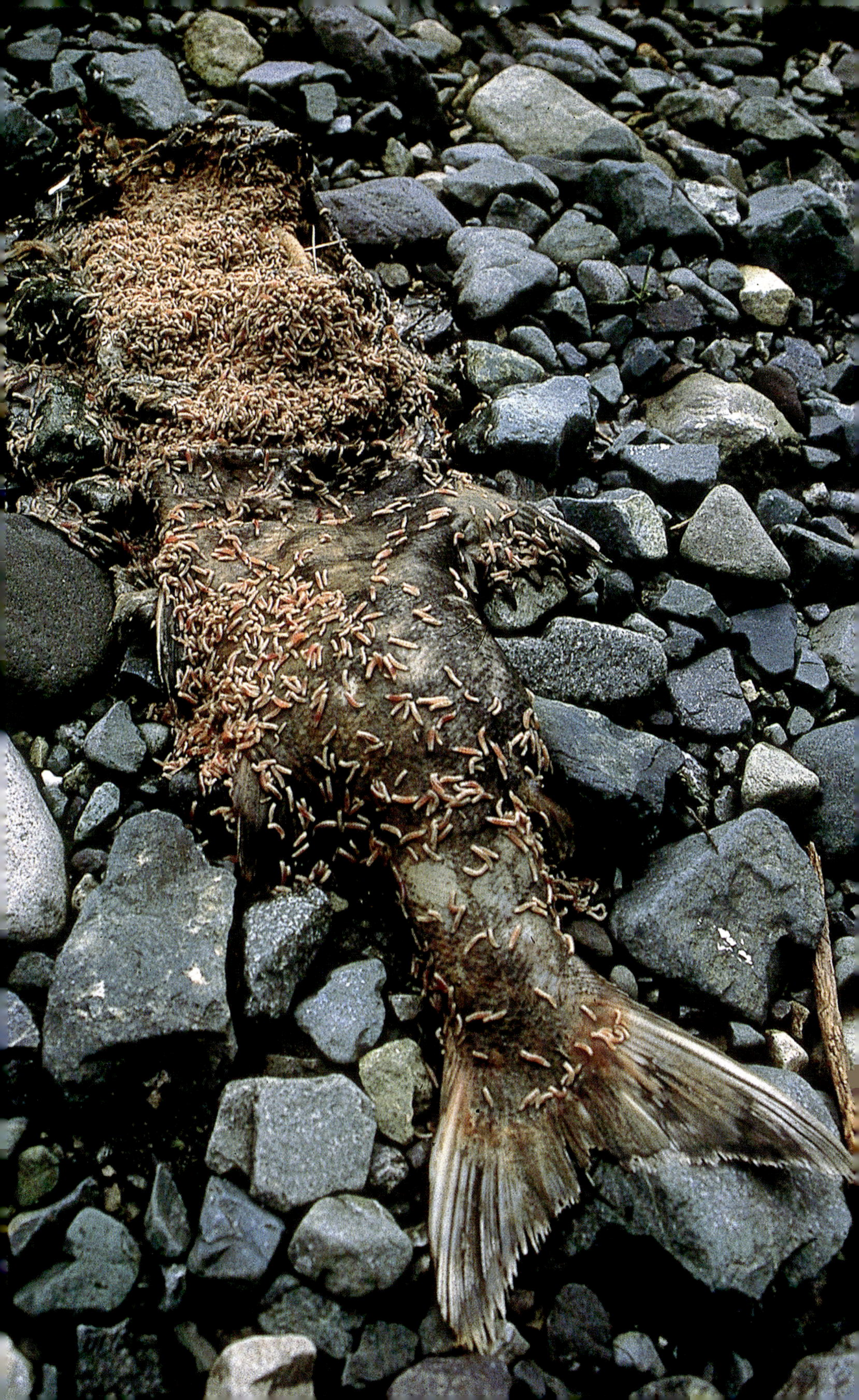

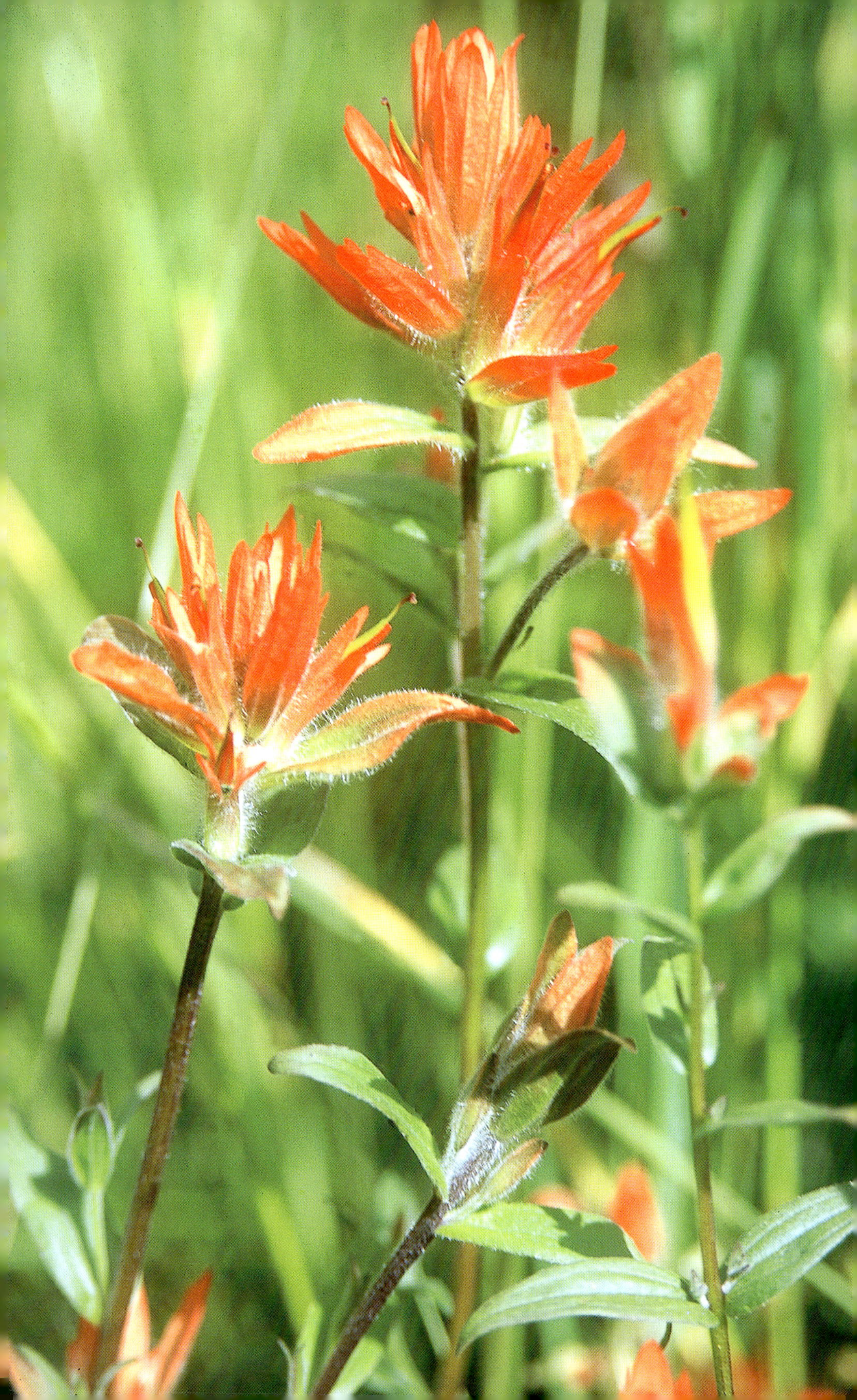

IN CONCLUSION

It is hard to overestimate the importance of salmon to trout fishermen in the Pacific Northwest. The decaying adults provide the nutrients that feed the insect life we imitate with our dry flies and nymphs; their eggs, flesh and offspring provide a rich source of food for the trout we angle for; and the rivers, forests and valley bottoms we draw so much pleasure from fishing in would be barren, lifeless places without the miracle of the salmon's gift of its body. The magnificent spectacle of thousands of spawning red and green sockeye or humpbacked pink salmon is impressive enough in themselves, but takes on a whole new meaning when you come to appreciate the salmons' contribution to our freshwater environment.

Matching the salmon hatches in each stage of their cycles is a rewarding and satisfying endeavour for all fly-fishermen, not just because it helps us to catch our quarry, rainbow and cutthroat trout, and Dolly Varden and bull trout char, but also because it connects us to the intricately interwoven web of nature that we neglect at our peril.

Facing page: Indian paintbrush.
photo by Fred Seiler

ADDITIONAL FLIES

Match the Salmon Hatch

Epoxy Head Alevin

HOOK: Tiemco 300 nickel-plated #10
THREAD: Clear monofilament or 6/0 white thread
EYES: 1.5 mm silver stick-on eyes
BODY: Medium pearlescent mylar tinsel over Z-lon underbody
TAIL: A hank of John Bett's white Z-lon
WING: An equal thickness of white Z-lon
EGG SAC: Red-orange yarn

TYING INSTRUCTIONS

Step 1: Cover the shank of the hook with tying thread and return to the head.
Step 2: Tie in the white Z-lon long enough to create a tail and wrap the thread to the barb and back to the head.
Step 3: Tie in the medium pearlescent mylar tinsel.
Step 4: Wrap the tinsel to the tail and back to the head. Tie off and trim.
Step 5: Tie in a Z-lon wing even with the tail and tie off.
Step 6: Tie in the red-orange yarn under the throat to imitate the egg sac.
Step 7: Build up a head with thread and apply the stick-on eyes.
Step 8: Cover the head with 5-minute epoxy being careful not to let it run into the wing or yarn egg sac.

Hot-glue Gun Alevin

HOOK: Tiemco 300 nickel-plated #10
THREAD: Clear monofilament or 6/0 white thread

EYES:	1.5 mm silver stick-on eyes
BODY:	Pearlescent Angel Hair
TAIL:	Pearlescent Angel Hair
WING:	Pearlescent Angel Hair
EGG SAC:	Red-orange or pale pink hot glue

TYING INSTRUCTIONS

Step 1: Cover the shank of the hook with tying thread and return to the head.

Step 2: Tie in the pearlescent Angel Hair to create a tail and wrap the thread to the barb and back to the head.

Step 3: Tie a hank of pearlescent Angel Hair long enough to make a body.

Step 4: Wrap the Angel Hair to the tail and back to the head. Tie off and trim.

Step 5: Build up a head with thread and apply the stick-on eyes.

Step 6: Cover the head and body with clear hot-glue gun glue.

Step 7: When the body has cooled, create an egg sac by using red-orange or pink hot-glue gun glue under the throat of the fly.

Gummy Minnow Smolt

HOOK:	Short shank nickel-plated hook in sizes 6-10
THREAD:	White 6/0 or clear monofilament
UNDERBODY:	Mother of Pearl Sili-Skin over lead wrap
BACK:	Road Slick Sili-Skin
OVERBODY:	Mother of Pearl Sili-Skin
EYES:	2.5 mm pearlescent stick-on eyes

TYING INSTRUCTIONS

Follow the instructions for tying Blane Chocklett's Alevin pattern, except for using the larger hook and adding an underbody of lead wire to weight the fly.

Hot-glue Gun Eggs (The Moe Fly)

HOOK:	Short shank gold-plated egg hook or any other short shank heavy hook
THREAD:	None or a red-orange thread to suggest the eyed eggs
BODY:	Five to six drops of red-orange, pink or peach hot glue gun glue

TYING INSTRUCTIONS

Build up a miniature "spawn sack" by adding one drop at a time of the glue.

Additional Flies

Hugh Storey's Single Egg

HOOK: Short shank egg hook or any other short shank heavy hook
THREAD: 6/0 black or pink thread
BODY: Medium salmon pink chenille
WING: A short tuft of white marabou to imitate the sperm

TYING INSTRUCTIONS
This very effective fly is simplicity itself. Cover the hook shank with thread and add lead wire if you want a weighted fly. Tie in the salmon pink chenille and wrap to the head, building the body up into an egg shape. Tie off and add a tuft of white marabou, if desired.

The Bead Egg Fly

HOOK: Short shank gold-plated egg hook or any other short shank heavy hook
THREAD: Red-orange wire or none at all
EGG: A red-orange, transparent plastic egg

TYING INSTRUCTIONS
Hollow beads can be attached to the shank of the hook with some red wire. Solid beads can be attached very effectively by heating the shank of the hook briefly with a lighter and pushing the bead down onto the shank while it is still hot.

Yarn Flesh Flies

HOOK: Mustad salmon hook #3690 in sizes #4-#8 or any other large, wet fly hook
THREAD: Red-orange, pink or white to match the body colour
BODY: Large red-orange, pink or white chenille over a lead underbody
TAIL/WING: Egg sack yarn to match the colour of the body

TYING INSTRUCTIONS
Step 1: Cover the hook shank with thread and come back to the head of the fly
Step 2: Wrap the lead wire around the hook shank and tie in with thread
Step 3: Tie in the tail of yarn
Step 4: Take thread to the head and tie in a matching wing. Bring thread back to rear
Step 5: Tie in matching colour chenille. Wrap body to "wing," and tie off